The Fat Pigeon Flies

*An autobiography of the Sheldon Community
celebrating 21 years of the Society of Mary and Martha*

Carl Lee
Sue Lee
Hillary Hanson
Sarah Horsman
Jan Kaye

The Society of Mary and Martha, Sheldon, Devon

First published 2007 by the Society of Mary and Martha
Sheldon, Dunsford, Exeter EX6 7LE

www.sheldon.uk.com

ISBN 978-0-9556384-1-1

A catalogue record for this book is available from the British Library

Printed by Phillips & Co, Crediton

The Fat Pigeon Flies

Contents

Come to the edge.

We might fall.

Come to the edge.

It's too high!

COME TO THE EDGE!

And they came,

and he pushed,

and they flew.

Christopher Logue

Selected Poems published Faber & Faber Ltd

for Steve Thompson

'All good fun'

Introduction

Many years ago, Sheldon had a new logo. It was a beautiful white dove flying into the dawn, symbolising peace and the Holy Spirit. It soon acquired the nickname the 'fat pigeon', and as such nicknames do, it stuck. The logo was used on our leaflets, prayer cards and letterheads for many years. It survived Church Army attempts at corporate branding and held its own alongside the Mary and Martha logo nicknamed the 'two fat ladies' until the early part of this century. It then made way for the 'Sheldon lozenge'. But the fat pigeon wasn't beaten yet, and when we needed a name for our licensed bar, the fat pigeon stepped in.

The fat pigeon seems to us an unlikely hero. Not graceful and pristine and pure like a dove, but pecking about in the dirt and struggling to get airborne because of the size of its belly. We like that as a metaphor for our own story - an unlikely group of people, neither especially holy nor especially gifted, doing something improbable together.

You won't find God mentioned and credited on every page because that sort of talk is not our style. We are, however, very conscious of God's leading and God's provision as the ministry of Sheldon has unfolded. We invite you to look for God between each line in the unfolding of our story. Our ministry is not primarily one of evangelism, but one of witness through service. Many people tell us that they discover at Sheldon a God who is easy to find even, or maybe especially, when we may be struggling to find God ourselves.

People often ask 'When did Sheldon start?' It's not an easy question to answer because there have been several stages of starting, and we usually stumble over an explanation of changes in ownership, personnel and ministry over the years.

We have chosen the occasion of the 21st anniversary of the founding of the Society of Mary and Martha in 1987 as the excuse to write the book. But our story goes back further than that – to Carl and Sue arriving here in 1976, and to Geoffrey Fraser buying the farm from the Sercombes in 1967. Living with old buildings and farmed land we are also conscious of unknown forebears through many generations.

The 21st birthday of Mary and Martha happens to have fallen on our watch,

ABOVE: The original Sheldon 'fat pigeon' dove logo.

and we are also the longest serving members in Sheldon's history. Those are our credentials for writing this book. It is necessarily our story with all the biases and selective memory that entails. No doubt there are others with different, perhaps less flattering stories to tell.

We are aware that we hold many hundreds of stories about guests who have entrusted us at Sheldon with a part of their journey. Some scandalous or fascinating, many painful, all unique. Those stories are, and will always remain, confidential, and do not form part of this book.

We have decided on various conventions in the writing of this book. Carl and Sue Lee, Hillary Hanson, Sarah Horsman and Jan Kaye are the members of the Community at the time of writing. 'We' refers to us now, and/or the composition of the Community at the time referred to. The five of us are referred to by Christian name only throughout the book.

Much of the story comes straight from our own memories, supplemented by our personal diaries, photograph albums, trustee minutes, archives of leaflets and newsletters. We know how slippery memory can be so we've cross-referenced with written records when possible. It has been disappointing to discover how much of our early archive material has disappeared, and how hard it is to date some events and photos. We have tried to be accurate, but will be pleased to correct future editions if you find errors.

We have included photos with lots of people. We have largely assumed that you can recognise the five of us, and have included names of as many others as possible where we have room and can remember who's who. If we have time, fuller captions and more archive photos will be added to our website. If you have photos that you would like to add to the archive, please do send them to us.

The hardest part of writing the book has been keeping it short. Most paragraphs could be chapter, and every chapter could be a book in its own right. We have tried to focus on what we think you might find interesting. We hope that you will enjoy reading our story as much as we have enjoyed living it. Perhaps you would like to be part of the next 21 years?

ABOVE: The Mary and Martha 'two fat ladies' logo.

LEFT: The Sheldon 'lozenge' logo with the cross and shadow from the medieval chapel.

Who we are

We begin by introducing some of the key players and giving an outline of the many groups of people who have been involved in the creation and development of Sheldon.

The Lee's first year

Carl and Sue arrived in September 1976, fresh from four years of Church Army ministry on a housing estate in Brighton. Sheldon had been running as a residential centre for nearly ten years since Geoffrey Fraser bought the farm for the Christian Discovery Association. He was under pressure from both the bank and the Charity Commission, and was trying to find ways to keep the project afloat. Advice was sought from CORAT (specialists in charity management) who recommended approaching the Church Army to recruit a resident Warden to be seconded for a year. Carl was looking for a move, and had expressed an interest in work with holidaymakers. Church Army Chief Secretary Donald Lynch put Carl's name forward to consider the Sheldon appointment. Carl understood the post would include some caretaking of Sheldon plus outreach work with holidaymakers within the Exeter diocese. Unbeknown to him, Sheldon was not considered to be in good standing, and it was to be fifteen months before its reputation was turned around and Carl was licensed for work in the diocese. Having arrived, and without permission for any other ministry, Carl had no option but to knuckle down and focus his attention on running Sheldon itself. It gave him an enduring appreciation of how hard that elusive quality of good reputation is won, and how easily lost.

By the time Carl was appointed, Geoffrey Fraser was working on

BELOW: Carl with Sarah Lee, Hilary Niblett and Catherine Fraser holding Melody ~ 1977

another project in Tiverton. He would come down to Sheldon for the weekly Wednesday morning Communion and stay for breakfast. Geoffrey has always tended to polarise opinion, with some considering him an inspired visionary, and others regarding him as a rogue or worse. At Sheldon he is remembered with great fondness for being immensely pastoral and kind to the Lee family as they unexpectedly found themselves in the centre of a conflict zone. The management committee was pulling in several directions at once. The local Harvesters group based at Sheldon had a different set of priorities, and was not best pleased to make way for the new arrivals in the Farmhouse. After a huge and fond civic send-off from Brighton, it was a lonely time having to navigate through so many different agendas, as well as being uprooted from the support of family and friends.

Norman Davey was Chairman of the management committee that was responsible for decision making at Sheldon. He was a tall, warm Devonian priest in the parish of Central Exeter, and director of education for the Exeter diocese. The committee had helpfully sacked all the cleaners on the day of Carl's appointment, leaving him and Sue to do all the cleaning of the buildings, and launder all the bedding. As the committee's schemes became increasingly impractical (building a windmill, setting up a butterfly farm, and putting a dovecote on the Long Barn were some of the more memorable), Norman came to the rescue with his characteristically practical and wise counsel. He put Carl forward as secretary to the committee, and once elected the pair of them then forgot to call any more meetings. This happy arrangement allowed Carl to focus on getting on with the job in hand until the Church Army bought Sheldon in 1977.

Colin Ward served as Warden at Sheldon before Carl, and he lived with his wife Chrissie in the old Woodshed, with what was then a startlingly stylish and modern interior. Colin saw Carl through the first couple of months of his new job, and is fondly remembered as a real godsend. For the first few months Carl and Sue had no car, so Chrissie would take them shopping in Exeter – a very practical gesture of friendship. Even after they had moved to Tiverton, Colin returned for a while

LEFT: Carl and Sue with Donald Lynch in London in 1972.

BELOW: Geoffrey and Mary Fraser visting Sheldon in 2004

to help Carl draw up the first plans for the theatre.

David Hamer and Geoffrey's daughter Catherine Fraser were Sheldon's maintenance team. Eighteen year old Catherine was on her gap year before training as a vet, and Carl soon discovered what a capable woman she was. David Hamer made regular visits to the newly formed Findhorn community where he learned to grow eye-wateringly large vegetables. Legend has it that he would hug his cabbages in the back garden. June Willoughby from Dunsford provided secretarial help, another real gem who was very kind to the Lee family in practical ways.

BELOW:Phil Hutchins below the Long Barn with Hereward and Bootle ~ 1980

The founding Sheldon Family

At a time when it was not making property investments, the Church Army made the surprise decision to buy Sheldon from Geoffrey Fraser in 1977. For the first time there was money to pay salaries, of £1,500. Mike Gardener and Guy Pierce were the first on the payroll, and with Carl and Sue The Sheldon Family was formed on 3rd October 1977. Mike, in his early twenties, had visited on a houseparty over Easter the same year, and stayed on camping afterwards. He was keen, practical, and good at bluffing his way through any challenge. His first project was to take down the trees by the entrance drive that had fallen victim to Dutch elm disease, and use them to create a play structure. He left to train at the Church Army college, returning later for one more year as deputy warden before being commissioned. He first met Kate Elkins as a young guest on another Easter workparty. They married in 1986 and continue to visit Sheldon with their son Oliver from the parish in Winchester where Mike is rector.

Guy Pierce was already living in the farmhouse south wing and was a member of the Harvesters, and a lay reader in Dunsford. After a rocky start things took a dramatic new course when Guy came in one Sunday night and asked Carl if he was serious

about this theatre idea, and joined the Sheldon team. He gave up his teaching job at Queen Elizabeth School in Crediton to put his acting training to good use as the first director of the Sheldon theatre company.

Over the next fourteen years of Church Army ownership, people found their way to Sheldon through a range of well-trodden pathways. Chief among these were Christian Service Scheme volunteers, Church Army students and officers, roadshow crew and the local youth group TYCIA. Some people joined the team for a few weeks or months, others made a longer commitment as a member of the Sheldon Family, attending Family meetings etc.

Christian Service Scheme

The Christian Service Scheme was a Church Army project for young people giving a year to God. Volunteers came to Sheldon for placements of three to six months. Between them they contributed a great deal of practical labour with varying degrees of skill and enjoyment. Tasks included feeding, putting out, putting in and mucking out the goats, donkeys and hens. They helped with cleaning the buildings, doing the laundry, running repairs, digging trenches, and building things (whatever was the latest shed, wall or other project on the go). There was laughter over ignorance of country skills - the girl who thought nettles were de-activated once pulled up so she sat on a pile of them in her shorts; the lad who

LEFT: Mike and Kate Gardner celebrating their 10th wedding anniversary at Sheldon in 1996

LEFT: Jim Pilkington and Sarah on workparty teabreak ~ 1982

ABOVE: Church Army Roadshow press photo in 1983. Nuala Forsyth, Sarah, Kate Elkins, Theresa Cockman, Maggie Bennett, Chris Cockman, Paul Welch, Carl, Martin Joss, Jon Moore, Jon Bicknell, Paul Tyler, Paul Cockman, Admiral Sir Horace Law.

Jonathan describes as 'an 'orrible caravan' near the main carpark. It was cold and damp with a hole in the floor in front of the sink, and he wondered what sort of godforsaken place he had landed up in. One girl lasted a record 48 hours - she arrived on Friday and was gone by Sunday. Many of those who did stick it out are now in ministry and still in touch with Sheldon. Phil stayed on after his CSS term and courted local girl Karen Peters. Phil and Karen were each employed at Sheldon at different times in the early 2000s and Phil continues as a member of the theatre team each summer. Jonathan remembers the sheer variety of tasks, learning to knuckle down and do things he didn't like, working as part of a team, and growing up. 'You couldn't expect to be mollycoddled, but Carl would always be there for you when you needed him'. He learned a lot about himself through practical work embedded in a discreet spirituality - not often spoken about, but always there underpinning everything. He remembers the shared sense of humour and merciless teasing; Carl and Sue making him welcome in their home; and the environment where people could talk about issues in their lives without fear of being judged. The seedling of Mary and Martha was already taking root, and 25 years later Jonathan is a priest in Wales and serves as chair of trustees of SMM.

didn't know what kindling was let alone how to chop it; the girl sent out to pick a cucumber from the garden but thought it was a root vegetable; the lad who was successfully conned into urgently fetching rat poison to deal with 'a nest of rats eggs' in the hedge (the hen who had laid them was rather surprised.) Depending on the time of year they would also help with children's clubs, beach missions, firework displays, theatre, etc. CSS volunteers included Paul Robinson, Phil Hutchins, Paul Hinds, Claire Chadburn, Jeanette McLaren, Neil Roper, Neil Sheppard, Paul Taylor, Robert Medford, Jonathan Williams and Steve Murphy. Accommodation for most was in what

Jim Pilkington arrived on his bike in April 1978. He stayed until September and then joined the Christian Service Scheme, later returning to Sheldon as maintenance man living in the Woodshed. After leaving Sheldon he put his practical skills to good use running a handyman service and serving as virger at Heavitree church in Exeter, while continuing to volunteer on Sheldon workparties and the theatre team.

Students and Officers

For a while, Sheldon enjoyed a bit of cachet as a desirable placement for Church Army students. It was widely known in the CA because of its appearance in the official slide shows and films of CA work around the country. These placements were usually four to six weeks long as part of their three year training based in London. Being trained for the office of evangelist, they would be expected to take some leadership responsibility in missions and children's clubs run by Sheldon – leading worship, giving their testimony, leading bible studies and house groups, telling stories and organising games for children, as well as Sheldon routine jobs like the CSS volunteers. Students included Pat Gower and Stephen Colver. When Carl was appointed as a Church Army assessor, a post he held for nine years from 1981, it was less appropriate for him to have students on placement. His role as assessor, along with one other from the CA and two from ACCM (forerunner of the Church of

LEFT: Claire Ward, Tez Hastings and Paul Welch as Flashpoint ~ 1985

BELOW: Steve Thompson driving the dumper truck, with Carl and Phil Searle.

RIGHT: John Hall by Farmhouse porch ~ 1968

BELOW: The job advert designed to catch Hillary's eye in 1982.

England's Ministry Division), was to assess each student and the college as a whole. It involved trips to London for several days twice a year. Stephen Colver returned to Sheldon in 1979, immediately after being commissioned

---

Sit. Vac.

SECRETARY/PERSONAL ASSISTANT to the WARDEN OF SHELDON

start work on Jan 1st 1983

Living-in job. Very odd hours. Even odder boss.

Dealing with wide variety of situations covering whole spectrum of Sheldon activities.

Salary and accomodation available.

Must be competent and willing to live a very different sort of life.

If interested, see Carl

---

and marrying Alison. They lived in the newly purchased mobile home and then moved into the South Wing when Guy and Fran Pierce left. Their two sons Rowan and Patrick were born at Sheldon. Stephen enjoyed the challenge of learning to lay hedges and keep sheep, and was keen on meditation. After leaving he trained as a psychotherapist and later served as a founding trustee of SMM, and chaired the trustees for several years. Barry Amis was the next occupant of the mobile home. He helped with the theatre, the Christian arts festivals, and the first year of the roadshow. He set up Radio Sheldon in a little caravan where he acted as presenter, director and producer of home grown music and chat shows.

TYCIA and other Youth

TYCIA (Teign Young Christians in Action) was a youth group set up for the Teign valley young people in March 1979. The prime movers were David and Pat Cockman in Bridford and Reg and Rosemarie Canvin in Christow – each with four teenagers in their own families. Meetings were held at Sheldon on Sunday nights with the usual youth club mix of music, talks, testimonies etc. There was some serious local alarm at the level of fundamentalism among its members (although not emanating from Sheldon) and Carl was summoned by Christow PCC to account for the goings-on. Sadly there was a good deal of bad feeling that lasted for many years. People who first came to Sheldon through TYCIA included Sarah Horsman, Paul Cockman and Chris Cockman. Sarah joined the maintenance team for her gap year in 1981 but lasted a whole two weeks before the rest of the team was fed up with her bossiness and she migrated to the office. She continued to live at Sheldon through her medical training in Bristol, and returned full time in 1987. Chris was maintenance man for several years, a member of the roadshow team, and left an enduring legacy in many stone walls around Sheldon.

Roadshow Crew

Every summer of the Church Army roadshow a fresh crop of keen young volunteers arrived on the scene, recruited through adverts in magazines like Buzz. Although their primary role was touring and preparation for touring, they also got involved with summer activities at Sheldon, including the theatre. Some of those who first came for the roadshow and later lived at Sheldon were Steve Thompson, Paul Welch, Claire Ward, Tez Hastings, Neil Wilson, Suzanne Reilly and Jenny Herbert. Steve Thompson drove the bus, came back as maintenance man and later became a founder member

of the Sheldon Community. Neil Wilson also served as a member of the maintenance team. Paul, Claire and Tez lived in the old Woodshed and formed Flashpoint Theatre Company doing music and drama in the local area. Claire and a friend filmed and directed the Mary and Martha promotional video in the summer of 1990. Tez later married Gail Bruce and they served three years as members of the Sheldon Community.

Other routes in

A few others don't fit into any of the above categories. Andy Leigh turned up with his parents and brother one afternoon when his Dad was a vicar in Plymouth. He stayed for his gap

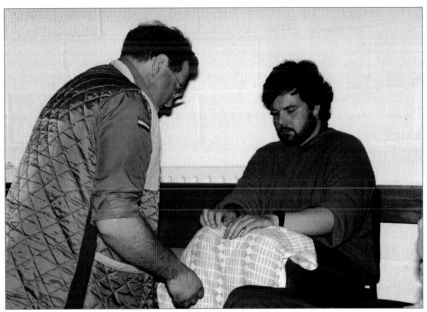

BELOW: Steve Thompson and Phil Searle - Maundy Thursday handwashing ceremony 1992

year in 1983 working mainly with Mike Gardner. Phil Searle was put in touch with Sheldon by Pat Gower when he dropped out of university at Bristol. He lived in the mobile home with Steve Thompson for a couple of years before going on to ordination. He and Claire Collins were married at Sheldon and they still return regularly

ABOVE: Housekeeping team July 1996 – Jan, Gail Hastings, Hillary

for workparties. Hillary was leader of a youth group in Crediton and was bringing a party to the Seedpack youth weekend in September 1982. Carl got Sarah to do a sit vac postcard advert for an administrator, reckoning that it might catch Hillary's eye. It did indeed, although she originally thought it would involve the occasional few hours at a weekend while she kept her day job. Peter Walker was a friend of Gibson Pattison, then vicar of Dunsford, and loved looking after the animals. David Turpin helped with early SMM administration in 1990/91, around the same time as Lesley Blythe moved to Christow in order to volunteer full time.

Sheldon Community Founders

When SMM bought out the Church Army in 1991, the Sheldon Community was formed, replacing the Sheldon Family. It consisted of Carl, Sue, Hillary, Sarah and Steve Thompson. Steve looked after the animals and grounds and worked on the cleaning team every changeover day. He was a gentle giant with a shy, almost dour exterior who claimed he 'liked children but couldn't manage a whole one'. Underneath he had a very dry sense of humour and a warm heart. His kidneys had failed from inherited polycystic disease and he had received a prompt transplant for which he was always profoundly grateful. He became increasingly breathless during the autumn of 1992 and early the next year he was diagnosed with non-Hodgkin's Lymphoma. He was admitted to hospital to have his spleen removed, and we geared up for the ensuing months of chemotherapy. Tragically, the lymphoma proved to be much more advanced than anyone had realised and he died aged 34 on 18th

March a few days after the operation. It was a huge shock and the four of us remaining were plunged into mourning. We cancelled everything on the programme for a month to give ourselves space to grieve and gather our wits. As people so often report in such circumstances, support came from many wholly unexpected quarters, and failed to materialise from some where it should have been forthcoming. Steve's coffin was welcomed into the Chapel of Christ the Servant for a few hours before the funeral service at Exeter crematorium. This was conducted by Derek Atkinson who was chaplain to Sheldon at the time. With invited friends, we scattered Steve's ashes in the theatre on Easter Sunday, and then tucked into his favourite lunch of sausage and chips.

Community members

For many years Tez and Gail Hastings expressed an interest in joining the

Community but were unable to sell their bed and breakfast business in Exeter. They finally arrived in 1995 and lived in the mobile home with their boisterous dog Harley. Gail took on housekeeping and catering duties, producing many delicious meals, and Tez worked mainly on grounds and maintenance. He also set up the studio for music recording in the animal barn annexe. They moved to Newton Abbot in 1998 to pursue further studies in media and food technology. Tez continues his involvement as a member of the theatre team, and helping with design and technical support for the Sheldon website.

Jan was put in touch by Sally Sheppard when they were both working with

ABOVE: Opening of the theatre burger bar July 1987. Includes Jeanette McLaren, Mike Gardner and Kate Elkins.

LEFT: Sheldon Community rededication in marquee July 1997, including Tez and Gail.

the homeless at St George's Crypt in Leeds. Like many enquirers before and since, Jan's first taste of Sheldon was an Easter workparty, and she has been a member of the Community since 1996. She had previously worked with the Mission to Military Garrisons in Cyprus and the Falklands. At Sheldon she joined Hillary and Gail on the Housekeeping Team. After Gail left Lindsey Bolton was put in touch with us by Rev Dr Una Kroll, one of our Patrons. Lindsey was convalescing from a life-threatening liver disease and originally came to live alongside the Community, working on a part time basis. She lived in Parrots' End (named after the chorus of squawking from Coombes Cottage at parrot feeding time) and then moved into the farmhouse porch bedroom. At the end of a year her health was much

improved and she applied to join the Community. She brought a lively presence to the kitchen and bar, and had a special relationship with the chickens, until leaving in 2004 to take up work as a care assistant in Exeter. She continues as a regular face behind the Sheldon bar at special events and in the theatre.

Bob Smith responded to an advert in the church press for someone to join the Community and work on the admin team. He arrived in 1999 as the first occupant of Mary's Lodge. As a single parent, he claimed the children had left home in Spalding so he had decided to do the same. Bob was a keen tecchie, and during his time in the office he set up our in-house payroll system among other things. He took a particular interest in Sheldon's liturgy and put together several of the chapel offices that continued in use for many years. Bob moved to Exeter in 2001 after a period of ill health and currently works in medical records at the hospital.

Renie Campbell did not end up joining the Community, but as part of the enquiry process she and her King Charles Spaniel Charlie spent six months at Sheldon during the long hot summer of 1995. Having recently retired from British Nuclear Fuels she came with capable organisational and computer skills. Sarah was away on sick leave for several months and Renie covered many of her admin responsibilities during this time. Sadly the vicar at her home church in the Liverpool diocese died suddenly and as the lay reader she felt committed to return and support the parish through the bereavement.

Alongsiders

Various other folk have lived alongside the community at Sheldon, sharing in our life and work, but on a short term basis and without the intention of taking on a community commitment. They became known as 'alongsiders', and for many of them Sheldon was part of a transitional period when life had taken a bumpy turn through ill health. Judith Ware lived here in 1992-3 after leaving work at Selly Oak College due to ME/CFS. She did a lot of catering and drew up our first set of maps for local walks that are still very popular with guests. She went on to Rydal Hall and then ordination.

Nina Joyner was a school friend of Hillary's who approached us when she needed somewhere to recuperate from exhaustion from service with CMS in the Gambia. She was the first occupant of Parrots' End. With her ecology skills she prepared the information board for the copse and botanical lists of the woods and meadows. Her long time admirer Clive

Summerfield finally caught up with her and they now live in mid Devon with children Nicholas and Timothy. Hillary is Godmother to Nicholas.

ABOVE: Community in 1999 including Bob and Lindsey.

Ann Buxton was living in Budleigh Salterton having taken early retirement from General Practice with depression. She joined the housekeeping team for a year from Easter 2002. Her star turns included surgery on a sheep after an unfortunate accident involving a fence and a horn. She now lives in Exeter and serves as a trustee of SMM and as a reception volunteer.

Mary Allaby lived alongside in the porch bedroom for eighteen months

2005-6 in transition out of parish ministry due to a breakdown.

Mary Weatherley was our only part-time alongsider, and also the longest serving. She and her cats regularly commuted between Parrots End and their home in Exmouth until Mary retired at the age of 70 in 2006. Mary presided at most of our community eucharists and we appreciated her willingness to fit in quietly and without fuss with the community's simple worship routines. She also worked in the kitchen and gardens and arranged flowers for the chapels.

Volunteers

Sheldon continues to depend heavily on the varied contributions of volunteers. Workparties have always

been a fantastic way of getting together to achieve great things. Sometimes there has been a big project like painting a new building where volunteer labour saves the charity lots of money in a very visible way. A lot of trenches for cables in the theatre were dug by hand on early workparties, and all our hedges have been planted and weeded by volunteers. At other times we concentrate on the less glamorous but no less important tasks of routine maintenance of grounds and buildings. We all discover muscles we didn't know we had, but many cheerful hands make light work of otherwise soul-destroying jobs. David Silk, Roy Walford, Ian Parker, William Parker, Cathy Sanderson, Peter and Jacky Ward, Mike Loader and Kevin and Janet Scott, are among many who have returned for further punishment at regular intervals.

As soon as we started running our own programme events like 12,000-mile

service weeks we needed hospitality volunteers to help with everything from cooking to leading walks and workshops. Hospitality volunteers from all over the country soon became vital members of the Sheldon team, usually offering one or two weeks each year. Many volunteers come first as guests and then want to give something back. Others are recruited by friends who think they would enjoy being involved in this way. Guests give a lot of feedback about how much they value the loving care and attention volunteers offer to guests. In the early days we felt somewhat apologetic begging people for help, but realise now that when volunteering works well it works for everyone. People frequently say they receive as much as they give. Recent regulars include Margaret Smith, Shirley Raynes, Tom and Ann Comley, David and Caroline Windsor, Freda Beveridge, Jeremy and Mary Allum, Lesley Barrett, Sue Wollen, Allan and Tricia Bapty, John and Dot Tesh, Jean Smith and many, many more. A special long service award goes to Roy and Norma Walford who have volunteered practically every year from the very first 12,000-mile serivce. Roy has also given long service as a trustee and chair of trustees.

The next new volunteer role came with the opening of reception in the Great Barn. Since 2003 reception volunteers have offered a friendly and practical welcome at the threshold to Sheldon. The squad has included Mark Churcher, Ann Buxton, Averil Swanton, Pauline Mortimer, Sheila Atkinson and Penny Hale.

Occasionally someone has a month or two to offer as a volunteer and if we have accommodation available this can work well. Liz Bellamy offered two stints on the housekeeping team between posts, the latest in 2006.

Some people with gardening or handyman skills enjoy the challenges of helping to keep Sheldon looking good and running smoothly. John Hall, Maurice Price, Jill Halliwell,

ABOVE: Painting the Linhay during July workweek 1998

ABOVE: Staff training on
use of fire extinguishers
January 2005

Esther Donne and Clare Bryden are among those who have helped to keep it weeded, planted and repaired. John's Sheldon connections go back to 1962 when he joined the Bridge Quest led by Geoffrey Fraser who was living near London and looking for a property where a group might develop their own prayer life in order to teach others. When Geoffrey moved to Dunsford and bought Sheldon, the Quest evolved into the Christian Discovery Association. John was one of its six committee members and moved here in 1968. After two years the association was moving in other directions so John left, and was later ordained.

Local staff

When the Church Army pulled out in 1991 money was very tight for a few years and Sheldon was run almost entirely by the Community and volunteers. As things have grown we have become a significant local employer with a dozen part time staff regularly on our books, and more in the summer months. Carl has a good eye for talent-spotting and when the Christian Education and Resources Centre in Exeter closed in 1993 Sheila Atkinson who worked there was recruited to the Sheldon office team. Soon after Sheila retired at Christmas 1999, Tracy Wilson moved to the end of the Sheldon lane and she has worked in the office since then. It is becoming a family affair as her son and daughter landed holiday jobs at Sheldon in the summer of 2007. Karen Hutchins, Penny Green, Sandra Parker, Paul Cochrane and Maryon Avery have all made their mark in the office. The books have been kept by Ann Ofield, Mary Wylie and Karen Cronin.

On the housekeeping team, cleaners have always been vital players on changeover days keeping the place spick and span from top to bottom. The longest serving members are Sandy Robertson, Anne Bricknell and Jacky Bryant. Deborah Ough and Ann Wilkinson both work as regular assistants on the housekeeping team.

Maintenance of Sheldon buildings and grounds is always a challenge, and especially when there is no resident member of the team with this particular responsibility. At least these days most equipment is fairly modern and we can afford to pay for specialist engineers. Carl certainly does not miss the years of the Friday routine of battling the ageing and temperamental boilers into action ready for the weekend guests. Local staff who have contributed on the maintenance team include Charlie Long, Sarah Russell, John McGahey, Rom Dobbs and Simon Lee. In the summer months the team is swelled by local school leavers or students home from university. Phil Cribb, Giles, Justin and Peter York and Thomas Partridge are among many who have mowed the grass, set up the theatre, and helped with summer projects.

Our apologies to any who have been missed out. There are so many people who have lived and worked at Sheldon as part of the team over the years. The general consensus is that whatever else a stint at Sheldon is, it usually manages to be 'character building'.

LEFT: Volunteers painting the Long Barn during July workweek 1996.

Legal and financial

From 1977 onwards, the Sheldon Family was busy with its core work running Sheldon as a residential centre for church, school, special needs and youth groups. However, Carl's growing concern about the lack of care for clergy would not go away. Chapter five covers in more detail the core of the ministry we were so keen to develop, while this one traces the journey by which Sheldon eventually became the home of the Society of Mary and Martha in order to carry it out. People often ask where our money comes from so we outline how things have grown from the £200 we first put in from our own pockets in 1982 to Sheldon today with a value of £2m and an annual turnover of £300,000.

Setting up the charity

On May 18th 1983 Carl first met with a solicitor, Gordon Rice, about setting up a new charity. The initial meeting was rather discouraging, not least because costs appeared well beyond our means at that stage. As we set about working out how to get some money together, the vision for the charity was steadily firming up, and we were actively looking for a suitable property to be the mother house. The first place we looked at was St Augustine's Priory near Abbotskerswell, recently vacated by Roman Catholic nuns. Carl put in a bid of £100,000 but it went to a higher bidder. Okay, so we didn't actually have any money, but you have to start somewhere. Other Devon properties were Maristow House which had been gutted by fire, St Scholastica's Convent in Teignmouth, and the convent at Chudleigh. Surveyor Roger Hands regularly joined us on these wild

BELOW: Trustees signing the trust deed in the farmhouse parlour in 1987, including Stephen Colver, Kenneth Newing and John Perry.

goose chases and contributed a lot of free expertise. In 1984 we looked at Llangoed in mid Wales. It was in quite a dilapidated state, and again we put in a bid for £100,000. We still had no money to back the bid and it was turned down. However, soon afterwards we received notification of a grant for £250,000 from the Welsh Office for which Roger had applied. It was too late for us to buy Llangoed (which has since been turned into a sumptuous hotel by Laura Ashley's widower) but it gave our confidence an enormous boost - perhaps we could believe that a miracle might just be possible.

In 1985 Arthur Probert put together the legal side of our application to register as a charity. The Charity Commission was relocating, so we would get frustrating letters telling us to expect a reply in six months' time. The first meeting of the trustees-designate was held on 12th June 1986 and the Minutes note '£2,000 working capital has been accumulated by various money raising arrangements which Carl explained'. The records decline to shed light what the money raising arrangements actually were, but they included buying large bales of mistletoe in Somerset and selling them on a Christmas market stall in Exeter high street. Sarah also made regular trips to London to buy women's clothing, mostly catalogue surplus

or floaty Indian dresses from traders in Islington. She ran fashion shows for anyone who would have us. The day would involve packing the volvo estate full with clothing and rails, and spending the afternoon setting up the venue and getting volunteer models kitted out with a selection of outfits. The fashion show itself was run in the evening with varying degrees of glamour and sophistication, hopefully followed by lots of sales and less to carry home late at night. Anyway, the £2,000 raised was enough to pay the solicitors to set up the trust, put the trading on an official footing by forming a company, and even have a little left over.

One morning, just as he was rushing off to a meeting, Deaconess Kristeen

ABOVE: Sarah raising money by selling clothes, hanging baskets and pot plants on the lawn outside the chalets during a Sheldon open day in 1984.

The Society of Mary and Martha

Give us the resources and we can do the job

'You can't just prime a pump and then expect it to work efficiently for 40 years'

Wanted: Des. Res.

Break-through

Caring for people in ministry ... caring for people in mi

MacNair from Manaton telephoned Carl to say she wanted to make a gift. He was astonished to receive a cheque for £5,000, effectively tripling the newborn charity's assets.

The Society of Mary and Martha trust deed was signed and witnessed on 5th February 1987. Having staggered out of bed with 'flu to sign, Sarah is looking particularly peaky in the photograph recording the great day. The original trustees were Carl and Sue, Sarah, John Perry, Stephen Colver and Kenneth Newing. The deed had been altered during correspondence with the charity commissioners - apparently 'the principal difficulty had been with the use of the word 'spiritual' '.

Looking for a home

Meanwhile Church Army had convened a review group to look at the future of Sheldon. Philip Johanson, head of the mission department, was expressing concern that the group had 'failed to deal with specific issues and make real recommendations'. In the autumn of 1987 Carl floated some ideas for SMM with the Church Army. These included everything from outright purchase of Sheldon by SMM (for £175,000), to SMM leasing Sheldon from the Church Army for a peppercorn rent of £1 year for 25 years. Detailed proposals included putting a reception, shop and conference facilities into the Great Barn, a covered walkway past the chalets, eight self-contained units in the Linhay, extension of the woodshed and south wing ends of the Farmhouse, and further facilities 'for example a swimming pool'. The proposals were rejected, and it seemed that SMM would have no future at Sheldon.

Learning to ask

Two years later we were still regularly scanning the property pages of

Country Life and were impatient with our slow progress in raising money for a mother house. We approached fundraising consultants Landire in the summer of 1989 saying we wanted help with 'selling our product, writing good copy, telling people what we do because we are too embarrassed to, and raising new money'. According to their report 'an appeal for £500,000 has been launched but with limited success to date ... the only detail associated with that appears to have been a statement that existing facilities are inadequate and a building with twenty or more bedrooms is required. The product which is being sold here is both a service and its new packaging but better definition is needed. A clear picture needs to be drawn and communicated to show what is to be undertaken in this new centre.... If a clear and detailed plan can be developed and costed the appeal for funds will have much greater credibility.' We had produced a little booklet about our ideas with help from a grant from the Christian Initiative Trust. Landire described it as 'attractive and informative but not good appeal literature ... generally lacks impact'. The covering

LEFT: The Sheldon Family in January 1991, including Simon and Sarah Lee, David Turpin, Neil Wilson and Steve Thompson. Taken behind the Farmhouse.

ABOVE: The hastily prepared Home at Last appeal leaflet from February 1991.

appeal letters were described as 'not sufficiently well written to inspire trust administrators to a substantial response ... it is not a question of poor grammar or technical inaccuracy, but of style and impact'. A detailed five year strategic plan was recommended complete with timetables and budgets. The resources needed to undertake the work were deemed to be 'not currently available from within the Society and it will be necessary to buy in some help to mount an effective campaign.' However, we baulked at the £500 quoted for a five day commission to work things up further, and especially at the recommendation to employ a salaried fund-raiser thereafter. We reckoned we could learn.

Our next effort was to convene a support group on April 3rd 1990. In February we prepared a booklet with everything from budgets to programme proposals. We invited the trustees plus twenty friends from various walks of life, and Anne Eyre to Chair the day. Participants were invited to read the document, tell us what impression it gave, and offer advice on future development and the finding of a house. A note in Carl's handwriting tucked into the file says 'Document has failed to do its task. We do not present the <u>need</u> at all well'. The key messages that came out of the day for us were 1) nobody seemed to have read what we had prepared, so we needed to raise our game on making promotional material attractive and accessible, and 2) the professionals like solicitors and accountants said our finances were in cloud cuckoo land and basically our dreams were an impossibility. This surprised us as we had used real figures for the running of Sheldon in our budget projections. Of course history proved them wrong, and several had the decency to come back and say so.

The problem of effectively communicating the need continued to dog our efforts to raise funds. Clergy stress simply did not have even the limited recognition or understanding that it has today.

Our assets were slowly creeping up, no doubt thanks to 'various money raising arrangements', with total assets of £12,800 by March 1988, £21,500 by March 1989, and £30,000 the following year. We invested £5,000 in 1990 running a four page advertising spread in the church press, raising our profile, promoting the 12,000-mile service weeks, and advertising our need for a home base. By mid 1990 we had 170 Associates and Friends. In theory Associates had a bigger commitment including turning up to the Annual Eucharist, but this never really worked so we continued with Friends only.

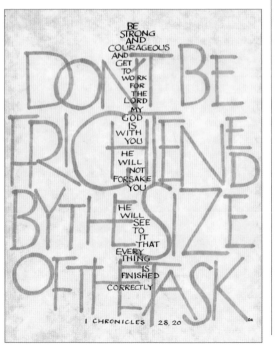

In October 1990 Carl reported to the trustees that a number of redundant vicarages in the Exeter diocese had been explored, including Chulmleigh, but none had proved suitable. He said he would probably write to the bishop asking if his offer of help with a loan might be extended to non-church property. We had spent £800 on a survey of Malmesbury Abbey being vacated by the Community of St Andrew. A local businessman offered to start the appeal with a donation of £100,000, but there were too many strings attached and the restrictions of a Grade I listed property with a garden listed as an Ancient Monument were very daunting. However, we were saving money at the right time with interest rates soaring to 15%. People were being incredibly generous considering there was as yet so little to show for the vision. In the six months to October 1990 £18,000 was donated by individuals and £3,000 by churches.

Buying Sheldon

January 28th 1991 was Carl's day off and he went shopping in Exeter with Sue. On his return he was summoned to the office for an urgent phone call setting up a meeting at Sheldon that Friday with the Church Army's chief secretary, personnel officer and finance officer. By Tuesday Carl had a pretty clear idea of the content of the meeting, and acted swiftly. We

LEFT: Calligraphy poster created for us during the appeal by Derek Atkinson. It hit the spot for us just right, and still hangs in Carl's office.

ABOVE: Children from St Nic's Newbury at Sheldon. In 1991 the children staged a concert for their parents who were not allowed out of the hall until they had contributed £1,000 to the Sheldon appeal.

had £71,000 in the bank. If Church Army was pulling out, maybe Sheldon itself was to be the Mary and Martha mother house after all? We spoke to trustees by telephone, had a hasty meeting with the local planning officer and ran off address labels for everyone on our database. We didn't have desktop publishing ourselves, so in great secrecy Sarah was dispatched to design a leaflet on Tony and Pauline Mortimer's computer at Pinhoe Rectory. By Friday we had a firm proposal in place. The Church Army had plans to close Sheldon in just six weeks' time, but we made a counter-proposal to run Sheldon for them on a break-even budget for six months. That way CA had nothing to lose, existing bookings would be honoured, and it might just give us time to negotiate a price and raise the necessary money. They agreed, the Mortimer's printing press sprang into action, and by Monday our appeal leaflets 'Home at Last!' were in the post to hundreds of supporters. We felt it was essential to seize the initiative and hang onto it for dear life. It would have been so easy for whisperings to take hold that 'Sheldon's closing down, Sheldon's over' which could have proved very hard to counter.

A meeting with the trustees was hastily convened on the 19th February. It was a highly anxious time, especially for Carl who was facing the very

real prospect of redundancy and homelessness with a disabled wife and teenage children. Maybe that wasn't so well understood by some who thought the decision to launch the appeal should have been taken with formal consultation and consideration of other options. The minutes record 'a great deal of hurt was expressed by those concerned over various mis-communications that seemed to have passed...' It was eight long years since our first bid for St Augustine's so we couldn't see that something else was suddenly going to fall into our laps. We had everything to lose by delaying, and reasoned that even if the Sheldon appeal failed it might set us up for buying somewhere else. Two trustees resigned and the appeal went ahead.

We appointed Roger Hands to negotiate for us, notwithstanding the irony that Roger was a former chief surveyor for the Church Army. We originally thought the asking price might be as high as £350,000, so we were secretly highly relieved by a final figure of £210,000 plus £10,000 for fixtures and fittings. We set an appeal target of £250,000 in the hope of avoiding ending up with a property but completely broke and unable to pay the bills. By May we really began to believe buying Sheldon was going to happen, and started to put structures in place. As trustees could not be employed by the charity, Carl, Sue and Sarah all resigned as trustees and Sue Wollen and Derek Atkinson were appointed in their place.

The Sheldon appeal was supported by so many people in so many ways, and responses touched us deeply. Opening the post was the nervewracking highlight of the day - we never knew what would be in it. Beryl Yates decided to forgo a trip to the Holy Land and give Sheldon the money instead - she had been a guest on the very first 12,000-mile service. Gerri Sharpe who we had never met sent a cheque for £5,000 (to be followed by several more in later years). Margaret Branch wrote a storybook and gave Sheldon the proceeds. Every morning before school Simon would go to his Dad's office and anxiously ask if there was enough money yet. By July, 350 individuals, 110 church congregations, fifteen trusts, and six religious communities had contributed. The Clothworkers' Company gave £10,000 and Smith's Charity £25,000. These were amazing sums for us. Paid adverts in the church press cost more than they raised, so we courted free publicity wherever we could get it. As we have now learned to anticipate, any financial appeal that raises the profile of the ministry also brings a heavy workload of requests for help, so it was a frantically busy summer. The contract with the Church Army was signed on the morning of the AGM and Annual Eucharist - 13th July. Carl was in full flow and he promised 'plans for development of the Sheldon site early in 1992'. Sarah dashed off straight after the service for her sister's wedding in the next village.

Carl kept a record in his journal of the monthly totals in our bank account

end February	£85,812
end March	£113,343
end April	£141,393
end May	£156,209
end June	£206,065
end July	£248,419
end August	£255,216

Paying ourselves

So we did reach the appeal target of £250,000, and didn't start our new life completely broke. But there

BELOW: Press photo for the We are Staying party August 1991.

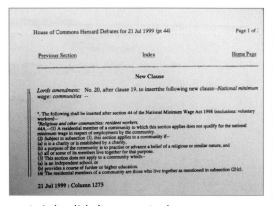

House of Commons Hansard Debates for 21 Jul 1999 (pt 44) — Page 1 of :

Previous Section — Index — Home Page

New Clause

Lords amendment: No. 20, after clause 19, to insert the following new clause--*National minimum wage: communities* --

*. The following shall be inserted after section 44 of the National Minimum Wage Act 1998 (exclusions: voluntary workers)--
"*Religious and other communities: resident workers.*
44A.--(1) A residential member of a community to which this section applies does not qualify for the national minimum wage in respect of employment by the community.
(2) Subject to subsection (3), this section applies to a community if--
(a) it is a charity or is established by a charity,
(b) a purpose of the community is to practise or advance a belief of a religious or similar nature, and
(c) all or some of its members live together for that purpose.
(3) This section does not apply to a community which--
(a) is an independent school, or
(b) provides a course of further or higher education.
(4) The residential members of a community are those who live together as mentioned in subsection (2)(c).

21 Jul 1999 : Column 1275

certainly didn't seem to be money available for salaries. With all the naive enthusiasm of pioneers we awarded ourselves food and housing plus the princely sum of £25 per week. The issue was brought into sharp focus when the National Minimum Wage appeared on the horizon in 1998. The law would be framed very tightly to avoid people being coerced into being low paid, and it would not be possible to get round it by saying we volunteered for it, or by deducting large board and lodging values. Did we have a principled case, or were we no better than any other exploitative employer? Sarah formulated a set of criteria for what became known as Intentional Communities and set about contacting lots of other groups to find out if there were enough of us to make a case for exemption. We found about twenty - retreat houses like Lee Abbey and Othona, new age communities like Findhorn, Buddhist retreat houses, Emmaus and l'Arche

communities, etc. We all lobbied our MPs, made submissions to the Low Pay Commission and tried to steer a tight path both supporting legislation to protect the vulnerable, and making the case for a principled exemption. A large meeting at the DTI in London was attended by communities from all over the UK. We were expecting movement, but the civil servants told us we were wasting our time - the law would have no loopholes and we had to work out how to live with it. Many bishops seemed squeamish about being seen to support our case - we assumed they must therefore be willing to see us and other similar ministries go under. In the end it was the intervention of Findhorn's MP that led to our case being made effectively at Westminster, and at 5pm on the day before NMW came into law we received a phone call to say that an exemption would be made. We were disappointed that some of the anti-exploitation principles embedded in our campaign failed to make it through to the final Bill. However, we had achieved the rare distinction of an amendment to flagship primary legislation that has made it possible for communities like ours to continue. Members of the Low Pay Commission came to breakfast at Sheldon on 24th June 1999 as part of a fact-finding tour - we don't know what they made of this unusual group of low paid workers.

Living on a very small personal allowance has never been easy for us, but we do it because we believe in what we do. For the first few years we did not have national insurance contributions paid, but then found we could inflate our allowance into the NI bracket, pay the stamp, and make a notional deduction to bring it down to our actual allowance received. The inland revenue told us it made a pleasant change to find people who wanted to buy into national insurance rather than doing their best to avoid it. For a while it cost about £1,000/year for the class A contributions, but then chancellor Gordon Brown changed the thresholds and gave it to us for free. In 2007 our basic allowance of £80 per week finally made it into the NI bracket without the device of a notional deduction, and we've even started paying a few pence of income tax.

Pensions are not easily come by for the low paid. For a long time it was only possible to put a percentage of your pay into a pension fund, in our case around £600 per year. Nonetheless we began making small pension contributions in 1997, and it helped the lower paid when the stakeholder pension arrived uncoupling pension savings and wages. The dilemma is that as things stand our contributions will be effectively wasted because of the income support

for poor pensioners. We can afford a decent quality of life day to day, but we have not found it possible to save adequately for our retirements. We have found it much easier to encourage people to give to visible things like building projects, than to people costs like wages and pensions. It can be hard when people ask for bursaries when they are probably much better off financially than we ourselves in the longer term.

We have chosen to put a proportion of our allowances into a pooled community account. We give 10% away, save together for holidays, cover big health bills and throw the occasional party. There is also a bit of charity money ring fenced to enable the trustees to make a discretionary

BELOW: Trustees in the Woodshed viewing plans for the Linhay in November 1993. John Perry, Tricia Bapty, Val Hawkins, Roy Walford, David Chance, Sue Wollen, Stephen Colver.

contribution to resettlement costs when community members leave.

Annual budgets

A key contribution to keeping us afloat in the early years from 1991 was a pump priming grant from

The Linhay

Linhay. (rhymes with mini). An open-fronted barn providing shelter for animals. With your help, the Sheldon Linhay will soon be helping us to provide shelter and open-hearted hospitality for people.

Events like the popular "12,000-mile Service" weeks are already demonstrating what the Mary and Martha ministry can achieve. We have seen hundreds of men and women rested and refreshed, returning to their ministries renewed and revitalised. We see God at work in gentle but powerful ways in people's lives.

The Linhay conversion is needed to serve the many others who need us quickly in a crisis, or who need several weeks to recover from a breakdown in their physical or mental health. Such accommodation will serve a large proportion of the several hundred people who already contact us each year.

"After ten years in a hectic parish ministry I find myself on the brink of nervous exhaustion. My doctor says I need at least a month of rest. Being a vicarage, home is a very busy place making it impossible to relax. I've done my best over the years. I know I need to take a break. I want to be effective for the next ten years of my ministry, and need help and advice. I know the Linhay will be a great blessing for people like me."

"My husband and I have four children, and share a ministry in a large inner city church. We have so little time for eachother, our marriage is really showing the strain. He has threatened to leave, but I know we can work things out if we just have the chance. We desperately need a few days away on our own together and with the chance to talk things over with someone. The Linhay will make a big difference to couples like us over the years."

Be a brick and help us build ...

Sponsor a Linhay brick for five pounds

We need 50,000 bricks (give or take a few)

Linhay Appeal Target £250,000.

The Society of Mary and Martha
Caring for people in ministry

The Society exists to offer support to people in Christian ministry and their families at times of stress and crisis. Being an independent and ecumenical charity it is uniquely placed to provide effective help to those who need it most. Thanks to the success of its Sheldon Appeal during 1991 it now owns the Sheldon Centre in Devon. This provides the ideal base for the wide variety of services offered by the Society.

All our guests benefit from the presence of a caring resident community, the beauty and peace of the Devon countryside, and accommodation that is simple, but warm and comfortable. In addition we have developed an unparalleled body of experience on the issues facing those in ministry, and are always pleased to make time to talk with guests in person, or on the telephone.

Single storey apartment for disabled guests

Four self-contained apartments, with living room and kitchenette downstairs, and double bedroom with en suite bathroom above.

The Woodshed conversion already under way will include a room where we can meet and talk with guests in privacy and comfort.

Archway through to private garden

Sheldon is a converted farm with grade two conservation listing. The final conversion may well differ from this preliminary design.

the Jerusalem Trust set up by the Sainsbury family. £42,000 was spread over three years towards the costs of the community allowances, food and housing. We really valued this vote of confidence in us as the core people making the charity's ministry happen. It has generated a very strong brand loyalty to Sainsbury's although we have to confess to some recent

backsliding when only Tesco's can do home deliveries in our area. It helped us to believe in ourselves when other people demonstrated their belief in us in such a tangible way.

Every year we reckon that if we're still solvent at the end of the year we'll run for another one. In the early days we really didn't know if we could survive long term as a completely independent entity. Even with the salary sacrifice of the Community we have never seemed to be able to cover more than about 50-60% of our running costs expenditure with earned income. As a result we have always been dependent on the generosity of supporters just to survive.

Budget forecasts are always tricky, and it would have been hard to predict in 1991 which costs would stay fairly steady and which would rise dramatically. The table shows a handful of directly comparable costs:

	1992	2006
Insurance	£4,500	£13,500
Energy & water	£10,500	£22,500
Phone & postage	£4,500	£6,500
Staff costs	£7,000	£78,000

In 1992 only the Community was employed. By 2006 we were one of the biggest employers of part time staff in the Teign valley with three people in reception/administration,

two in housekeeping, four cleaners, three in grounds plus students in summer holidays. It's a big financial commitment to have a wages bill of over £6,000 per month. We estimate that an additional 4,000 hours of labour are provided by hospitality, reception and workparty volunteers each year, with a monetary value of over £25,000 at minimum wage rates.

Capital appeals

Capital appeals have to be made for every new building project. There have been a lot of appeals, but we won't bore you with the details of every one. Suffice it to say that each one starts from scratch, and there are never any guarantees. People often say 'oh, you're so good at fundraising' but we don't really know what that means. We all find it difficult to ask for money, but we have to put a lot of time and energy into doing so. We only start a project if we believe in it wholeheartedly. We have always made

a point of trying to enable supporters to be involved with a project through newsletters, prayer letters, progress leaflets, events, photos, etc.

In December 1996 a briefing paper for the trustees was prepared on the basis of Roy Peters' quote and monthly cash flow timetable for the Linhay. It noted '£36,000 will pay for demolition and foundations to damp course (2 months); £100,000 will get as far as putting the roof on (11 months). £200,000 will complete the building works (18 months). There is currently £21,000 in the Linhay fund'. The trustees authorised signing of the contract 'to begin on 14th April 1997, provided that EITHER at least £100,000 has been raised in cash or loans to get as far as putting the roof on; OR £50,000 has been raised in cash or loans to get as far as the damp course AND there is a reasonable likelihood of a further £50,000 being raised within 6 months'. The contract stipulated that we could interrupt work at any stage with two months notice. Every month we checked the funds to make sure we could pay the bills for the next two months. Sometimes we sailed very close to the wind, and the final cost including landscaping, fundraising and professional fees came to over £300,000. But the Linhay was built without having to stand the builders down.

LEFT: Foundations of the Linhay being poured in May 1997.

BELOW: Carl did a sponsored washing up for the whole of a family holiday week to raise over £1,000 for the Linhay appeal.

The building of the Courtyard was the project that had the potential to make the organisation, or to capsize it. The capital cost of £1m was five times our annual turnover. Unlike the Linhay, we had to take existing accommodation out of commission before its replacement could be created. Because of the long lead time for group bookings we had to make decisions a long time before the capital funds were in place, and weather the loss of income during construction. The Linhay was completed in the spring of 1999, and by June Carl was reporting to the trustees on preliminary consultations with architects and planning authorities for the Courtyard. An application was submitted in the autumn, and appeal patrons were recruited. In February 2000 we sent an appeal leaflet to all 2,000 people on our mailing lists.

A series of design meetings were held to work on technical details and specifications, but the timetable was slipping. By June the appeal had reached £80,000, but we were running out of time for an August contract signing to start in January 2001. The contract was prepared in three stages - the external shell of walls and roof, the interior of the Pound House and the interior of the Great Barn - again so that we could call a halt part way through if necessary. By August £140,000 had been given, pledged or lent, but this was not enough to commit to the first phase. Carl and Sarah outlined to the trustees the risks of getting stuck at the end of phase one, with an empty shell at the heart of Sheldon with no earning capacity. Balanced against this was the risk of doing nothing and seeing the fabric of the building deteriorate and require remedial expenditure. Roy Peters said he could wait until March 2001 for a decision about starting in the August, so we postponed. At the end of February there was £251,000 in the Capital Fund, of the £300,000 budgeted for phase one. We swallowed hard and with 'cautious faithfulness' the trustees signed the contracts in March. Sarah warned there could be no guarantees about fundraising for phases two and three. Most of the trusts that might give substantial amounts had already been approached for phase one.

Work began in July and in November the trustees needed to make a decision on phase two. Insufficient funds had been donated, but we were able to approve it on the strength of £60,000 worth of interest free loans. In May 2002 phase three was approved, again on the strength of loans, this time of £100,000 from the Exeter diocese.

We have found the hardest part of fundraising is the bit to pay off the outstanding debts after the actual building is finished and in use. It's much easier to say 'if you give then this will happen' than 'this has already happened please help pay the debts'. We finished the Courtyard with £80,000 still owing, and the Pig Pens with a deficit of £45,000. But in each case it was all paid off within a year. One supporter took great delight in writing a cheque for £11,000 to pay off the Pig Pen debt as she had been involved with so many building projects during her ministry and understood the slog of the final push. Another supporter has on several occasions opted to launch an appeal with a generous first gift into the fund of up to £10,000.

Mary and Martha Enterprises ran as a trading company with an arm's length relationship to the Society until the law was changed to allow charities to do a certain amount of direct trading. We wound up MME but within a couple of years circumstances changed again and we needed to set up Sheldon Ltd as a wholly owned subsidiary of the charity. The tax regime as it applies to charities can be quite complicated, and more so when listed buildings are brought into the equation. It is very easy to fall foul of VAT rules and a constant watch has to be kept on legislative changes.

Legacies

Receiving legacies is always very touching and very exciting. Their monetary value has often been, in our terms, very large at £5,000 to £20,000. Legacies cannot be

BELOW: The trustees signing the contract for the Courtyard construction in March 2001. Val Hawkins, John Perry, Averil Swanton, and Sue Wollen.

Sheldon Courtyard development

renewing a heart at the centre

(see page 59)

episode was when we were targeted in an early round of Nigerian fraud scams. Shortly after we produced our five year building plan (see page 59) with a budget of £617,000 we received a telephone call and then a fax notifying us of a £100,000 legacy from a former missionary. We put it in the hands of our solicitor who treated it as genuine, and tried not to count unhatched chickens, but of course it was very exciting and we had spent it five times over in our imaginations. A few weeks later Carl spotted a short paragraph in the Church Times explaining how a sharp eyed secretary at CAFOD had averted a £6,000 fraud scam, and the details were stomach-turningly similar to our 'legacy'. It was a crushing disappointment, but fortunately we had not parted with any money. These days the scams are much more widespread and everyone knows to be wary, but we were more vulnerable when it started back in the early 1990s.

Just as money raising has its lows, so it also has many, many highs. Since 1991, individual supporters have contributed 7,500 gifts to a total value of nearly £1m. In the same period, almost exactly the same amount has been contributed by a total of a hundred grant making trusts. Churches have given nearly £250,000 in over 2,000 gifts, and religious communities seventy gifts

ABOVE: First appeal leaflet for the Courtyard with typical reliance on Andrew Newland's artist's impressions.

budgeted for and they do not come in response to a specific appeal, so they often provide an opportunity to do something special. Frances Pollcock posthumously paid for half of Friends' Field in 1997, and Kenneth Jackson for a full refurbishment of the Long Barn in 2005. Some legacies are from people with a long association with Sheldon, but they can also come as a complete surprise from people we have never met. An unhappier totalling £40,000. Opening the post can be a huge and unexpected delight. We are immensely conscious of the wide network of relationships these figures represent. People who pray for and believe in what Sheldon is about. People who are willing to give, often sacrificially, to make it possible. People like Christopher Airy, Eric Dancer and Richard Eyre who have discreetly made vital introductions to trustees and grant officers of major trusts. People who have got on and arranged fundraising events without requiring any input from us, like Paul and Diane Harrison's strawberry teas and Rosemary Howell's concerts at Lukesland. People who remember Sheldon for gifts in memory of loved ones or to celebrate anniversaries, or to tithe an inheritance. The hundreds of faithful Friends who give regularly by the boring old device of standing orders that warm the cockles of a treasurer's heart. Every one of them are part of Sheldon's story.

LEFT: Unloading £30,000 worth of oak beams to be assembled into trusses for the Great Barn in February 2002.

Community life and work

We're a rather shy group of people, all introverts, living a rather public life, so we try to protect our privacy. We debated during the writing of this book how much of the tough stuff to include. The trouble is, it feels a risky thing to tell the world about our more personal struggles as past experience tells us that it can easily backfire. However, it would be neither true nor faithful to make our story sound charmed and trouble-free. The biggest difficulty is when people latch on to a chink of weakness and become quite insensitively intrusive. No doubt they are anxious to be helpful, but when complicated by their own agendas

BELOW: Sarah Lee inspecting the fire engines attending the March 1984 chimney fire.

and projections it can be a painful experience to be on the receiving end. So we have included, with some trepidation, what feels safe enough to put into the public domain, and the rest will wait until another day. This chapter is mainly about the interface between the day to day work of our ministry and our domestic lives.

The Farmhouse

The Farmhouse is a thatched building with a leaning porch and all the quirks of a 500 year old grade II listed building. When Carl and Sue moved in with their three year old daughter Sarah, the Farmhouse bathroom was accessed via the entrance hallway shared with the South Wing. The occasional guest would wander in the front door, either lost or curious, and on one occasion startled a heavily pregnant Sue in the bath. A keypad entry system fitted on the Farmhouse front door costing £300 in the late 1980s improved quality of life and privacy hugely. When Sue arrived home from hospital with Simon in April 1978, the proud father and grandfather (Sue's Dad, Fred Bunce) knocked a hole through the wall from the parlour to create a more

LEFT: The Lee family in the Farmhouse sitting room Christmas 1989.

private access to the bathroom. The new facilities were appreciated, but the district nurse was seriously unimpressed by the wanton creation of so much dust and dirt with a newborn in the house.

The Farmhouse parlour has an aga which originally burned solid fuel, and there was an open fire in the sitting room. Both required a lot of carrying and created plenty of dirt. The coal hole was in the dustbin area at the entrance to the courtyard, and the log store in the little yard behind the Farmhouse. Mr Borlase from Bridford delivered logs and we barrowed them round the back to stack them in the woodstore. Carl would split them with his axe on a platform outside the Farmhouse kitchen door, usually smoking his pipe, and muttering the names of anyone who had crossed him. When Chris Bovey rethatched the house in 1995 he said there was serious charring of the thatch around the chimney. Like a lot of Devon

houses, it probably signalled a narrow escape for its occupants at some unknown point. That was in addition to the known fires in the aga chimney in 1976 and 1984. The date of the first is sadly etched in Carl and Sue's memory as the day of the miscarriage of a much-wanted baby. The first central heating was put through the kitchen and bathroom in the mid 1980s. In 1999 Carl and Sue moved into one of the newly completed Linhay Lodges while the aga was converted to oil, central heating was extended right through the house, and an upstairs bathroom was installed. It was alarming in the process to discover just how tasty the death watch beetle had found the floor joists.

BELOW: Coffee time in the Farmhouse parlour. This photo mid 1980s but typical of any time until 2004.

ABOVE: Sarah's caravan in the old vegetable garden behind the Linhay ~ 2000.

BELOW: Caravan being moved into place in 1981 with the trusty dumper truck.

During the years when Sue's mobility was worst affected by arthritis, the awkward steps and stairs in the Farmhouse were a serious problem, and especially when she was briefly using a wheelchair and convalescing from a hip replacement in 1988. Fortunately her mobility has now improved, but it has served as a constant reminder to think about accessibility whenever we build new buildings.

Laundry

The Lee's domestic washing machine only lasted a few months coping with Sheldon's laundry as well as their own. For years the parlour was hung with 52 brown sheets and pillow cases twice a week on wooden concertina airers, unless radiators in the Pound House or Long Barn were available. It was a massive improvement when the Woodshed was opened in 1993 with high level sheilamaid airers, and the Abel Trust gave a grant to buy SMM's first commercial washing machine. Of course since then the laundry demand has more than expanded to fill the available space. After a big changeover you can barely squeeze through the laundry for the piles of dirty linen, and now it is the conservatory that is frequently hung about with drying washing.

Sarah's caravan

Sarah moved into an old green mission caravan by the vegetable garden in 1981. It had lovely wooden interior fittings, bench seats to sleep on, a portapotti in a cupboard and a tiny gas cooker. Chris Cockman created more storage space by building in a high level bed, and the wood burning stove was replaced with a gas heater. Keeping cool in the summer was often more of a problem than keeping warm in the winter, and the roof and windows developed terminal trouble keeping the rain out. Baths and meals were gratefully cadged from the Farmhouse on an increasingly regular basis. Sarah was the first occupant of the new woodshed flat in 1993, and revelled in having a real toilet, a bath, and central heating. The caravan was stripped down, the aluminium sold, and Mike Atkinson converted the chassis into a trailer to transport his wife's pony and trap. After twelve years the wheels still went round. The rest was burned, and went up like a box of matches.

The South Wing

Hillary commuted from Newton St Cyres for her first few months in 1983 and then lived in the porch bedroom for the summer before moving into the South Wing when the Colvers left. Her sitting room was regularly borrowed as a place for Carl or Sarah to meet people as there was no other suitable room until the Woodshed was built and Sarah's kitchen/living room became the favoured venue. In 1995 we extended the South Wing. The kitchen was doubled in size to create the Community kitchen, with a new flat above for Hillary. Hillary's old sitting room became a bedsit which Jan moved into in 1996. The new double

glazed windows, plus the conservatory added on to the front of the house made the place much warmer.

Kitchens

There was a serious shortage of kitchen space for a very long time. Whenever Pound House or Long Barn kitchens were not available, Sue cooked in the Farmhouse or Hillary in the South Wing, for theatre company weekends, roadshow crews or theatre performers like Pam Ayres or David Kossof. Cooking for anything up to thirty people in an ordinary domestic kitchen could be a real challenge.

There was great rejoicing in 1978 when Mrs Kahn's Trust at the Nat West bank in Exeter provided a grant

ABOVE: Simon Lee, Sarah, Carl and Chris Cockman working on the South Wing lawn in 1983.

LEFT: Sue in the farmhouse kitchen with a batch of pickled onions in 1987.

of £250 to buy the first freezer which lived in the Farmhouse hallway. Sue also shared the Farmhouse kitchen with Sarah in the 1980s for blanching baskets full of runner beans for the freezer or making vats of marrow chutney to sell. The Sheldon Family used to meet in either the Farmhouse or South Wing on Friday nights to batch cook for the freezer for shared meals. Chicken curry, fish pie and mushroom rissoles were our favourite regulars.

When we started the SMM programme events in 1987 all the cooking was done in the Long Barn. The kitchen had an awkward storage area with a

larder fridge whose door opened the wrong way so you had to squeeze past it before you could get the door open. All food supplies had to be carried up there when the event started, and cleared out when it finished. We had some shelves on the Farmhouse landing for dry goods, and sold any surplus fresh foods back to ourselves. In those days Sarah had a health-food fetish as yet untempered by an understanding of the need for palatability and digestibility. For a short time, she used the Woodshed for catering for smaller groups of up to six guests, but that involved a lot of moving furniture about. When the Community kitchen was built in 1995 it was brilliant to have a regular kitchen for catering. The downside was that this space was doubling for hosting guests and as Community domestic space. As our programme and numbers grew, those living in the South Wing especially felt the pressure. We knew that sooner or later we would need a solution that took

BELOW: Steve Thompson and Sheila Atkinson in the Pound House kitchen 1991.

LEFT: Community members toasting the spacious new Pound House kitchen in February 2003.

BELOW: Hillary in the old south wing kitchen in 1993. The cupboards are now in the workshop.

some of the pressure off our domestic quarters.

When we started sketching up designs for the Courtyard we allocated a decent amount of space for the kitchen. The first plan had the kitchen wrapped in a U-shape around the stairwell - we're glad that one saw the cutting room floor early on. It takes us back to the old problems of repeatedly having to clear out of the kitchen to make room for self-catering groups, but the alternative would be to run catering full time, or become so rich we didn't have to earn a living. Jan has built up her cooking skills over the years and patiently instructs ever-changing teams of volunteers. Freezers have sprouted in all sorts of places and at the last count we had eleven scattered in barns, sheds and kitchens around the site. These enable us to use garden produce through the year, have our own lamb and mutton butchered, and buy whole beef and

pork from local farmers. There is a constant supply of ready meals being cooked to provide stocked larders for Linhay and Pig Pen guests. These are either put by from cooking for the table, or batch cooked in the Community kitchen.

Offices

Offices have also been rotated and extended over the years. Carl first worked upstairs on the Farmhouse landing. Once the access to the Farmhouse bathroom had been sorted, he was able to make a little office opening off the Farmhouse hallway which he inhabited for a quarter of a century. Space was squeezed as Stephen Colver and Barry Amis joined the team making three desks and a filing cabinet in a room just eight feet square. Carl had a magnificent manual typewriter that still lives in the loft against the day when all electrical supplies fail for ever. A Gestetner duplicator lived on the Farmhouse landing and none of us miss those messy days of ink and stencils. Sarah's arrival on the team in 1981 meant that more space was needed. Her admin duties in the first year were

mainly concerned with the roadshow, so the little office tucked upstairs in the Farmhouse was known as the roadshow office for many years. It had a nice desk and a portable typewriter, but no telephone which was a bit of a disadvantage for an office. Hillary was Sheldon's first employed administrator and she worked in Carl's office for the first four years. Next a doorway was made from the Farmhouse hallway into the south wing sitting room to make a decent size office there. The fireplace and patches of green flowery wallpaper reminded of its domestic past for many years. Sarah also had a desk in there from 1987 onwards, and managed to be away on holiday when the ceiling fell down in 1996. Everyone else therefore got the task of moving the entire office into the conservatory until the ceiling could be replaced. The office was shared by many others including Tracy Wilson, Bob Smith and Karen Hutchins, so space continued to be at a premium.

When the Farmhouse bathroom moved upstairs we doubled the size of Carl's office so he had room for easy chairs for meeting with people. The advantage of the close quarters in the Farmhouse was ease of communication. The disadvantages were chronic lack of space and lack privacy for conversations and phone calls. The offices shared a front door with the Lee's home, and were in very close proximity to our living quarters. We managed for a long time, but were very ready for the move to the Courtyard when that was completed in 2003. Or so we thought...

When the longed-for move came it threw up some wholly unexpected challenges. Sarah procrastinated for weeks until she was finally lured by the coolness of the cob-walled interior versus the south wing office super-heated by the conservatory. It was many more weeks before Hillary finally saw the back of Sarah's clobber and was able to re-order the newly styled housekeeping office. It was a challenging few months getting the new Great Barn space working smoothly as reception and offices. Carl found the move even harder and didn't move in to his new office in the Great Barn annexe until early 2004. Once moved, his old office was converted into the Community 'gymnasium' where those of us who want to keep fit can work out on the exercise bike,

LEFT: Sarah putting together the desk for her new office in 2006.

LEFT: Carl in the small farmhouse office 1989. The cross on the wall was made from old oak from the farmhouse.

cross trainer, rowing machine or steps. Phil Searle says Carl shouldn't be given offices with a view as he always ends up looking out of the window and re-landscaping what he sees - it didn't take long before the new Pig Pens were in his sights.

Although Sarah's new office upstairs in the Great Barn was spacious and impeccably appointed she never mastered the challenges of hot-desking between there and reception below. Two years later Carl had the idea of knocking together an office store and toilet just next to reception. After a very dusty and noisy couple of months Sarah enthusiastically downsized and took happily to her new quarters.

BELOW: Sue in the Lean-to Stores ~2000. The wooden counter made by Adrian Canvin has migrated to become the Great Barn reception desk.

Shops

The first shop was in the Farmhouse hallway with large folding shelving made by Sue's Dad. The shelves saw service in many other guises after the shop moved to the old Great Barn lean-to. The Lean-to Stores were so called because we weren't quite sure whether the planning consent covered a shop, and we thought no-one could object to a store. It was spacious, but difficult to keep warm and dry, and Sue had to go round there especially to staff it. While the lean-to was being rebuilt as the current Great Barn annexe the shop returned to the Farmhouse hallway for two years, before migrating to its current location in reception. The space is much smaller but it gets more custom because it is staffed throughout the working day.

Storage

From the outside Sheldon looks like a big place, but trying to find room to put stuff is a constant struggle, and we always argue over who has rights over storage areas. Sue needs space for storing shop stock; Carl for theatre equipment, grounds machinery, and maintenance stuff; Sarah for archives and stationery; Hillary for gardening and food and animal supplies; and Jan for linen and cleaning materials. As well as the Woodshed laundry and store we have closely-guarded cubby holes under the stairs in the south wing, in the woodshed loft, on the Farmhouse landing, out in the potting shed and marquee store, up on the barn tallet and down in the wendy house. Supplies are locked away under the window seats in the Pig Pens and in various cupboards in the Pound House and Long Barn. No wonder our poor volunteers are so disoriented when asked to fetch something. In the days when the Great Barn was largely empty space, and especially while the roadshow lorry was under-employed, we ran a low-key unofficial furniture store and recycling service. The reputation simply grew by word of mouth as somewhere to send your old wardrobe or chairs, and they were given away, used at Sheldon, traded, dismantled or taken to the tip. Noticing the service we were offering, Exeter City Council even granted free tipping rights for a while.

Workshops have moved over the years from the back of the Great Barn, to an annexe built by Ernie Townsend along the back of the old Linhay, and then to the annexe of the Animal Barn.

Clothing

A guest once confided to Hillary that she would never be able to join our Community "because of having to share your clothes". The comment

ABOVE: Carl and Sue with children waiting to come into the hallway shop ~ 1979.

mystified us and then made us laugh. It turned out she had seen Hillary wearing a certain rugby shirt, and noticed Carl wearing the same one in a photograph. Just for the record, we don't have to share our clothes but they do sometimes rotate as cast-offs, as the rugby shirt had. When we traded in clothes there were often bargains that more than one of us

LEFT: Community doing our best to look glamorous for the barn opening party July 2007.

snapped up. We also get to requisition unclaimed lost property occasionally. When he first arrived, Carl regularly wore Church Army uniform all day, complete with grey 'battle dress' suit and white shirt and tie. Between us we have committed all the fashion crimes of the decades but also scrub up reasonably well when occasion demands. Carl has Gordon blood and enjoys hiring a kilt for special occasions. Jan has more flamboyant dress sense than the rest of us put together.

Family life

Connections with our own families are important to all of us. Jan's all live around Huddersfield which tends to mean a lengthy trek home to see them. She has a mother and two brothers plus a good selection of sisters-in-law, nieces and nephews. Her beloved older sister Sylvia died in February 2004 aged 49 after a long battle with skin cancer. Jan was able to fly home and help care for her during the final six weeks and was with her when she died.

Carl and Sue's families both come from Sussex where Carl has two brothers and Sue one sister. Both have faced the challenges of trying to care for and support elderly sick parents at long distance in their last years. Their children Sarah and Simon grew up at Sheldon and now live locally. Sarah is in Newton Abbot which is close enough for plenty of bonding between grandparents and grandchildren Charlotte and Sam. Simon has spent several stints living and/or working part time at Sheldon while he has studied for his degree and worked as the Dartmoor ranger for the Teign valley. He now lives in Hennock.

Hillary and Sarah both grew up in Devon and both have parents still living nearby. Hillary has one sister in Wales and another recently returned to Devon, and a clutch of five nephews and nieces, one of whom, Catherine Byrne, has already been proving an excellent recruit to the family holiday volunteer team. Sarah was thrown into turmoil when her younger sister Alice was killed in a farm accident aged just 38 at the end of 2003. The bereavement was further exacerbated by a host of legal and financial complications which took several years to resolve in her capacity as executor. Her niece and nephew live with their father in Dorset.

In sickness and in health

Day to day work at Sheldon requires a fair degree of physical and mental energy and stamina, but of course these are not always in constant supply. Sue has battled with rheumatoid arthritis and its complications (including hospitalisation for bouts of cellulitis and pulmonary MRSA) plus depression, for over thirty years, but at least is now successfully past her five year follow up for breast cancer. Carl has the scars to show from the removal of his gall bladder in 1981 and parotid gland in 2005. The latter was the reason for cutting off his trademark long curly hair and

giving up smoking his pipe, and left him with long term complications. He also contracted a severe septicaemia from a prostate infection but insisted on sowing the Pound House lawn the day he got out of bed. Sarah spent years trawling various alternative

LEFT: Jan and Hillary posing with cake ingredients in the Community kitchen for a Christmas Goodies flyer to promote the fundraising Christmas shop. August 2006.

and para-orthodox approaches to tackling below-par health and had five months off in 1995 with exhaustion/breakdown. Her physical and mental health finally improved by getting thryoid and adrenal hormone deficiencies sorted out. Jan has type two diabetes which of course requires a lifetime of careful management. Apart from a hysterectomy and back trouble, Hillary generally has the healthiest track record of us all. The female contingent also get the range of female complaints from PMT to hot flushes, and among us (male and female) we sport phobias of mice, rats, spiders, snakes and heights.

We have had plenty of opportunity to learn that life sometimes dishes up too much to cope with all at once, and that for whatever reasons God does not always answer our prayers for healing, however faithful and fervent. From our own experiences, we deeply appreciate the value of getting alongside and truly trying to understand and support people who are struggling through chronic illness, bereavement, stresses related to work or relationships, or other challenges. We have a rather deep rooted suspicion of pseudo-spiritual 'quick fixes' prevalent in some Christian circles.

Jobs and training

None of us were exactly trained for the jobs we do - most of our learning has been 'in service training', ie learning on the job. Carl apprenticed as a print compositor and then did his theological training with the Church Army. He has a certificate from the English Speaking Union to certify that he can speak proper, and did three years training in Clinical Theology. Hillary did a secretarial training at Exeter Technical College where she was top of the class for shorthand speed writing. She worked as secretary to a senior probation officer and then the county librarian in Exeter. Jan did a two year secretarial and clerical course and then worked as a machinist in a Yorkshire textile mill for ten years. Having long been interested in physiotherapy she jumped at the opportunity for a massage training, gaining her ITEC qualification in 1998. Sue did a secretarial training and worked in a solicitors' office. Sarah trained as a doctor in Bristol and left immediately after graduation.

BELOW: After several peripatetic years of setting up her massage couch in the woodshed or south wing sitting rooms, Jan finally had a proper therapy room in the courtyard development in 2003.

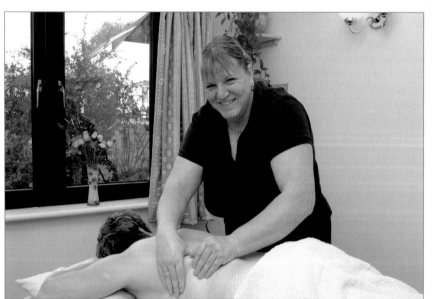

Our general attitude is to see what needs to be done and then work out how to do it, sometimes tutored under the watchful eyes of friends and volunteers. In the process we have ended up knowing more than we ever knew we wanted to know about everything from raising money to septic tank management; from theatre lighting systems to cleaning chewing gum out of carpets. The shapes of our own jobs have changed in accordance with the evolution of the ministry and the jobs of others on the team. Carl's level of hands-on work around the site has varied with the capability of the leadership and membership of the Maintenance team. Hillary and Sarah did a 50% job-swap around 1997. Hillary had inherited group bookings and other admin from Church Army days while Sarah was doing programme bookings and finance: Hillary was organising catering for workparties and Community, and Sarah for 12,000s and other events. There was ample scope for

duplication and friction until we created a housekeeping department led by Hillary and an administration department led by Sarah. The shape of both jobs and the working relationship were dramatically improved. Role differentiation has increased markedly over the years.

The advent of more specialist equipment from tractors to computers, the tighter legislative framework from food hygiene to health and safety, plus the growth in size of the organisation and our individual skill development, all mean we are more specialists and less jacks-of-all-trades than 21 years ago.

ABOVE: Jan, Sue and Lindsey enjoying the first plunge in the jacuzzi 2003. Not that we have spent much time there since.

LEFT: Hillary and Sarah in the courtyard on the day of the July 2002 Thanksgiving Eucharist.

The daily routine

We try to strike a balance between the different routines dictated by our respective roles and temperaments, and having a basic framework of shared common life. Carl is the earliest riser because he wakes early, and Hillary is next because her dog wakes her up. Before 8am chapel we have usually each had breakfast, Hillary has walked the dog and checked the sheep, Jan has let the hens out, Carl has unlocked the offices, Sarah has done a workout in the gym, and Carl and Hillary have each written a yard of lists for the day. We all join for prayers in chapel at 8am, and then between 8.30am and 9am staff arrive for work, the phones start ringing, and breakfast is served if we are running a programme event. We reconvene for coffee at 11am, with staff and/or volunteers and/or guests.

If we're running an event lunch for guests and whoever is joining them will be 12.30pm, but otherwise we do our own thing anytime from 12noon to 1pm. On Saturdays we share a bread and cheese lunch as a Community and on most Sundays Lee children and grandchildren join us for a cooked meal. We try and make time for a sensible lunch break including either a dog-walk, some horizontal back-care or contemplation of the insides of our eyelids.

There's a mug of tea on the go at 3pm and chapel at 5pm, followed by more dog-walking, sheep-checking, greenhouse watering (summer), gym workout (Carl), cooking supper if there's an event running (Jan), catching up in the office (Sarah), or opening the bar (Sue). We always have a Community meal together on a Saturday night, and this is an important part of our week. We try to balance the times when we are busy with a lot of evening commitments, with quieter times when we pack up soon after 5pm. We all enjoy our own space, especially if we have been giving out a lot of people-oriented energy during the day.

BELOW: Hillary feeding the sheep in the orchard in May 2007. The Manx lambs have a great sense of fun.

Days off can fall on odd days so it may be hard to see friends with more normal work commitments or sign up for regular extra-curricular activities. We all take holiday at Christmas and in the first half of September when Sheldon is closed. In the early summer we keep Sheldon running and stagger our holiday dates. Carl has discovered a late passion for walking kindled by a 60th birthday pilgrimage to Santiago de Compostela in 2007. Sue is a great knitter and many of her creations appear in the shop. Jan loves crafts and Hillary is big on rare breed sheep and being taken for walks by Lady. Sarah enjoys photography and digital imaging, walking and cycling.

ABOVE: Jan showing off the new henrun in the paddock in July 2007.

Buildings

The physical presence and character of the Sheldon buildings have played a formative role in the development of the Sheldon ministry. The quirky and characterful shapes of the old cob, stone and rubble walls, the simple friendliness of the whitewashed finish, and the soft contours of the thatched roofs all convey an immediate message to people arriving up the Sheldon lane. A cluster of separate buildings offers a different mix of independence and communality from a single large house. The buildings have probably shaped us almost as much as we have shaped them over the decades.

The Farmhouse, Chapel, Great Barn and Pound House are all grade II listed. The other buildings are all in their curtilege which means they too are subject to conservation planning restrictions. The Farmhouse is 16th century or earlier originally with a

RIGHT: aerial view ~ 1960. The basic layout remains familiar today. Like many similar farmsteads, a large number of apple and elm trees have been lost to age and disease.

cross passage layout but described in the 1975 listing as having a 'complex evolution'. It still retains some 16th century doorways and panelling and some very handsome dressed granite in walls and fireplaces. The Chapel is believed to be late 15th century, and the Pound House and Great Barn late 17th century. Changing fashions and personalities in the conservation field are sometimes hard to reconcile with the needs of 21st century occupants of the buildings and the necessity of staying financially solvent to run them. It is a delicate and challenging balance. When Geoffrey Fraser bought Sheldon from the Sercombes, many of

the farm buildings were in a sad state of repair. For the first year or so guests stayed in the Farmhouse.

ABOVE: The original 1960s conversion of the Pound House.

Early conversions

Architect John Deal designed the early conversions of the Pound House, Great Barn, Long Barn, Pig Pens and Chapel. He was ahead of his time in his commitment to conserve the original fabric of the buildings. Windows were placed at high level on the top of the old walls instead of cutting holes in the cob. Good for the walls, but making it harder to enjoy the view from most of the Long Barn and Pound House bedrooms. The original conversions were carried out on shoestring budgets, and often with volunteer

LEFT: A lean-to on the Great Barn interrupted the view of the Chapel.

RIGHT: Long Barn and Piggeries ~ 1966. In spite of the many developments, the shape remains instantly recognisable today.

labour. This achieved getting the centre up and running but left a legacy of Heath Robinson heating and electrical

RIGHT: The main room in the Pound House complete with remnants of the original cider press. The long screws were used as door lintels in several places. Billy Sercombe lost part of his thumb when the beam against the kitchen wall split.

systems and poor quality joinery that often proved expensive to maintain. The experience meant that when it came to our turn we were determined always to build to as high a quality as we could possibly afford in order to reduce maintenance costs. It hasn't always been easy to invest in a long-lasting standard when we have not known if we would have the funds to continue in business the following year.

One advantage of knowing Sheldon so intimately before we bought it was that we already knew all its weaknesses and foibles. We went in with our eyes

wide open. We knew that the Church Army had barely invested anything in the fabric beyond basic maintenance for the past fourteen years. The only construction project during their tenure was to replace the lean-to storage area behind the Great Barn with a shop and toilet block for campers. There was very little domestic accommodation for community, minimal catering, laundry or storage space, and no suitable one-to-one meeting space. There were problems with the access lane and the water supply. The guest accommodation had been designed for 1960s young people whose needs were very different from 1990s stressed adults. The quality of the guest accommodation was very basic with two large dormitories in the Pound House and bedrooms without central heating or an upstairs toilet in the Long Barn. On the plus side, we were already running events here, and knew we had the foundations on which to build.

The grand plan

In the years since buying Sheldon we have had building work going on somewhere on site for more time than the place has been a builder-free zone. Most of the construction has been carried out by Roy Peters and Sons, a small family firm in Dunsford. They have contributed enormously to Sheldon through their attention to detail, steady routines and willingness to embark on big projects in spite of our sometimes precarious finances. A bit of a joke has developed that Sheldon (and Carl in particular) just loves building projects, and we can't bear to be without one. It's true that there can be a nice buzz when a project is going well, and

LEFT: The original lean-to – replaced first with the camping Toilet Block, and then with the Great Barn Annexe.

BELOW: The Great Barn and part of the Pound House ~ 1966.

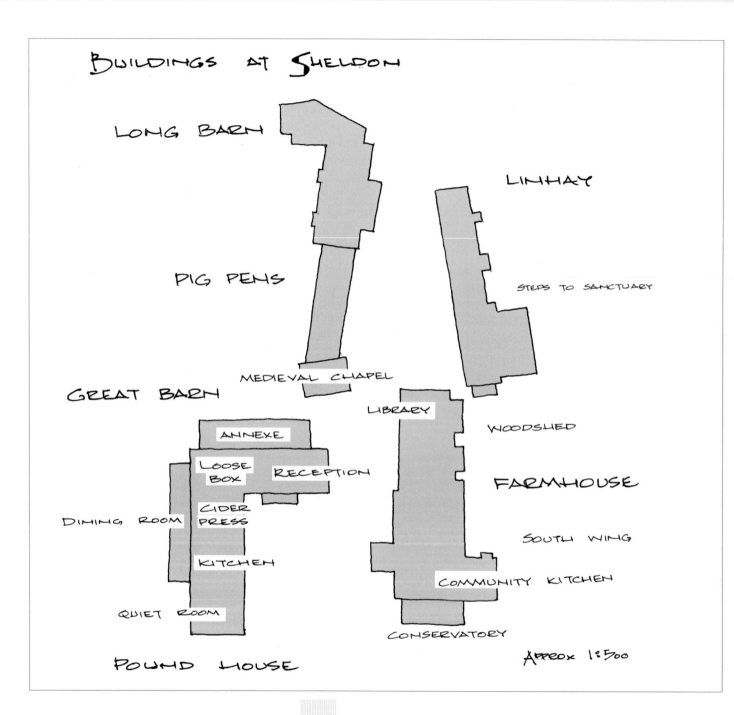

BUILDINGS AT SHELDON

LONG BARN

LINHAY

PIG PENS

STEPS TO SANCTUARY

MEDIEVAL CHAPEL

GREAT BARN

LIBRARY

WOODSHED

ANNEXE

LOOSE BOX

RECEPTION

FARMHOUSE

CIDER PRESS

DINING ROOM

SOUTH WING

KITCHEN

COMMUNITY KITCHEN

QUIET ROOM

CONSERVATORY

POUND HOUSE

APPROX 1:500

when we open something new that people admire and guests appreciate. The other side of the coin is a huge amount of work and stress raising the money, caring for guests through the disruptions, managing the projects and battling deadlines. We only build because we believe the needs of our ministry dictate it, and we don't embark on a new project lightly.

The first project, within months of buying Sheldon, was to refurbish the Long Barn and Pound House kitchens. The local environmental health officers were being particularly fierce at the time and had threatened a couple of local pubs with closure for kitchens with similar issues to ours. We installed stainless steel work surfaces, tiled the walls, put non-slip flooring down, and knocked out the horrible fridge alcove in the Long Barn. Within a couple of years the rules had eased a bit and we might have got away with less.

In April 1992 Carl presented the trustees with a detailed development plan. The summary page read:
'Woodshed   £60,000
Field   £27,000
Workshop/Animal House   £25,000
Linhay   £250,000
South Wing   £55,000
Great Barn   £200,000
TOTAL   £617,000
The first project begins in May 1992,

LEFT: Interior of the old Woodshed in 1992 with the pot-bellied stove whose burning coals caught Mike Gardner's washing alight.

and as long as the necessary funds are raised on target, we plan to complete all the works within five years.'

That original plan has been fully realised although it took us eleven years, cost nearly three times as much, and we added a few projects along the way. Perhaps our courage would have failed at the outset if we'd known how much of our lives would be absorbed by building works.

Decisions had to be made on the order of priorities. We were anxious

RIGHT: Half way through the re-building of the Woodshed. Sadly the cob walls had to be demolished, but it did at least make space for a bigger laundry.

RIGHT: The old Woodshed from the back garden after the willow tree was taken down.

that it didn't look good starting with Community accommodation and an animal barn before getting on to the guest-oriented project of the Linhay. However, there were logistical constraints on the order in which they could be carried out, the project management experience gained on the smaller buildings proved invaluable as we progressed to the larger ones, and there was a quantum increase in our workload when the Linhay finally did come on stream. For all these reasons we were glad of Carl's wise insistence that we didn't just jump in at the deep end with the Linhay.

The Woodshed

We cut our teeth on the construction of the Woodshed. The design was carefully planned around the existing cob walls which were part of the listed

building. It was designed to provide lots of resources that were missing - a laundry, a food store, a flat for Sarah, a toilet with disabled access, and a library/consulting room. Once the building work was under way we realised that not only did the cob walls have no foundations, but they were fragile shillet (crumbly stony subsoil) up to two feet above ground because the level of the yard had eroded over the centuries. In the middle of a hot and dusty summer we had to stop work, get a structural engineer to certify the walls unsound, and go back to the planning authority for permission to knock them down. The Woodshed was completed in 1993, enabling us to dispose of Sarah's caravan which was in the way of future plans for the Linhay.

The Animal Barn

The second big project was the Animal Barn. We needed somewhere to re-home the workaday contents of the old Linhay and workshop before we could rebuild the Linhay. Why not leave the old Linhay and build guest accommodation from scratch? Because we could get planning permission for a brand new agricultural barn, but not for new build residential accommodation. The barn was completed in 1995 and we don't remember any particular hitches. There is a universal law that states

LEFT: The Animal Barn under construction in 1995.

clutter will expand to fill the available space, and every year Carl gets in there with a team to have a thorough tidy up and throw out the accretions of things-that-might-just-come-in-useful-one-day-but-take-up-too-much-space-in-the-meantime. A decade later we extended the barn by another longitudinal bay as Sheldon's acreage had doubled and machinery and

BELOW: Adrian Canvin and Simon Lee barrowing in the concrete for the Community Kitchen foundations in 1995.

RIGHT: More concrete being barrowed in May 1996 for the conservatory floor, this time by Tez Hastings and Ben Seal.

BELOW: The summer 1995 workparty volunteers celebrate their achievements on the south wing extension. Including Peter and Jacky Ward, Tricia Bapty, Roy and Norma Walford, Paul and Diane Harrison, David Silk, Liz Bellamy, Roger and Sue James, and Jim and Margaret Sharman.

livestock had multiplied beyond the original capacity of the barn.

The South Wing

Extending the South Wing was next in our sights to provide a catering kitchen, a dining room large enough for us all to eat together and another unit of Community accommodation to enable us to grow. Money was very tight but we were keen to continue putting the pieces of the jigsaw in place. A two storey box was built adjacent to the end of the South Wing. Once the roof was on Hillary moved out for the messy knocking through to combine the old with the new. We were delighted with the lovely new Community kitchen - enough space for catering and a long table for sitting

and eating. Hillary's bold choice of dark green wild sage for the walls has been much admired and copied by many guests. Workparty volunteers in July 1995 painted walls, made curtains and completed the post-builders cleaning blitz. Hillary went shopping for light fittings during the week and came back saying she'd seen a lovely central pendant for the kitchen, but at £60 it was outside the budget. One of the volunteers promptly wrote the necessary cheque, and it made a lovely finishing touch. Hillary moved in to the new flat above the kitchen and soon afterwards Jan joined the Community, living in the newly created bedsit. The bills were getting paid, so the following year we added a conservatory to the front of the South Wing and everyone quickly migrated to enjoy a lovely gathering place. It was another year before we could afford the carpet for the floor and roof blinds to keep the temperature down in the summer. We very soon transferred catering for guests from the Long Barn

into the Community kitchen because it was so much more convenient, and we were able to start a bar for drinks before supper. Although the bar was tiny and operating out of a cupboard we still needed a formal alcohol licence. We went through the whole process of plans, advertising, police and magistrates' checks, and Hillary and Sarah had their day in court. With the licence granted, we then needed a name. A whole range of ideas were floated with a farmyard or ecclesiastical theme, but it was the Fat Pigeon who won the day. The Fat Pigeon lived in the South Wing for nearly a decade until s/he flew across the yard to the Great Barn in 2003.

The Long Barn

During the winter of 1995/6 we spent £80,000 on a major refurbishment of the Long Barn. The original conversion no longer met modern fire safety needs as escapees would have had to clamber out of small windows and down ladders at either end of the building. The two floors had to be properly fire separated, so the old gang-plank landing and open stair into the common room were replaced with a fire-protected oak staircase leading to the outside. When it came to measuring up we found that not one wall was parallel or perpendicular to any other wall so it was an interesting 3D exercise getting a stair built to

fit the space accurately. Most of the downstairs walls were just raw concrete blocks with paint on, and a smooth render throughout improved the appearance. Guests really hated traipsing downstairs past other people eating breakfast to get to the toilet, so we divided up the largest bedroom to give a much-needed upstairs toilet and shower. We were enormously proud of this logistical achievement but within weeks guests were politely regretting that there was *only* one toilet, and the occupants of chalet one were being woken in the night by mysterious

ABOVE: manhandling the new Long Barn screen into place.

LEFT: Adrian Canvin fitting the Long Barn staircase January 2006.

flushing from on high. The best bit was having warm bedrooms as the upstairs was centrally heated for the first time. The worst bit was putting Sarah in charge of the colour scheme – a duty she has not been asked to repeat, although she maintains to this day that pink and maroon doors are still better than the ubiquitous magnolia that went before.

The Linhay

Finally we were ready to start on the Linhay. We submitted our planning application, confident in the knowledge that the principle had been discussed with the planning officers before we launched the appeal to buy Sheldon five years previously. We were stunned

when the plans were not only rejected, but accompanied by a letter from the chief planning officer saying that no further development would be permitted at Sheldon. We would never have bought it if we had known, and would certainly never have spent the money on all the preparatory projects. Back to the drawing board. We reverted to Roger Hands as architect, consulted again with the planning authority, scaled down the design, and started gathering a portfolio of written support from neighbours and county dignitaries. We were obliged to go right back to basics and justify everything we were about. Why was new accommodation needed? Why here, and why with a resident staff? etc. It was a very worrying time. What we desperately wanted was to be able to respond to clergy who needed somewhere to go at short notice and/or for several weeks. The 12,000-mile service weeks were good, but for some reason people didn't seem to be able to plan their crises to fit in with our advance timetabling. The chalets were booked long in advance most weekends by the self-catering groups and so were only available for short midweek individual visits. We wanted the new accommodation to be spacious, and the space itself to have a healing quality. We wanted privacy from whatever else was going on at Sheldon, and the option of guests being self-contained so we weren't tied

BELOW: Hillary posing with the donkeys outside the old Linhay for a not very successful Linhay appeal fundraising effort. We were disgruntled that people seemed willing to give millions to stressed donkeys while we struggled to raise basic funds for stressed human beings.

to catering all year round. Many of the imaginative design features owe a debt to Beatrice Carfrae working for Roger Hands and already suffering from the brain tumour that would end her life not long after. Thankfully the design and the campaign were successful, and planning consent was eventually granted second time round.

We were so engrossed in the building detail that the results surprised even ourselves. The lodges were fantastic, and ten years later they are still among the best retreat accommodation in the country. It was not uncommon to show a guest into their lodge and realise they were in tears 'All this, for me?' Guests were profoundly moved that so many unknown others had cared enough about them and their ministry to make this space possible. Early feedback repeatedly referred to the way guests felt loved during their stay in a lodge. This surprised us if we had barely seen the person between arrival and departure. We were used to love being a quality of more direct personal hospitality and care. Slowly we realised that the love and care that had gone into creating the lodges, and continued

ABOVE: The nicer of the two Pound House dormitories in 2000.

BELOW: Design for the beds at a 1975 workparty. 'Big and heavy!! Tough. Of immoveable nature and much durability' - they did 25 years of service.

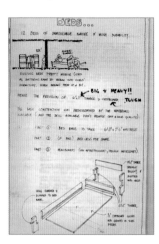

to go into the cleaning, stocking of larders and tending of gardens, was experienced genuinely by guests even when the contact was at one remove.

The Courtyard Development

By now we had gained a great deal of experience in managing building projects. Over the next few years we were to need every ounce of it to achieve the combined Pound House and Great Barn conversion billed as the Sheldon Courtyard Development. We were faced with obsolete 1960s dormitories and communal washrooms in the Pound House, and empty space in the Great Barn at the heart of the centre, housing just a decrepit table tennis table. We had no welcoming reception; the pressure on our domestic accommodation was increasing from the office and the kitchen as our activities expanded; bedroom, meeting and therapy space was at a premium; and repairs were needed to the Pound House. There was no half-way solution, we either had to go for the big one, or quietly retire from the fray.

Having had our fingers burned at the planning stages of the Linhay, we consulted carefully before putting pen to drawing-board. The conservation brief was basically 'no new holes in cob walls', which meant we had to design all windows and doors around existing openings. Initially it seemed

an impossible task, but we got there eventually. We wanted to link the Pound House and the Great Barn but we couldn't knock through the internal dividing wall, and we couldn't visually impact the central courtyard with a covered link between the two doors that way. Tez Hastings and Simon Lee suggested putting a conservatory along the back. We thought it was a very long shot, but with 'enlargement' of the window opening at the back of the Great Barn, and a design style we nick-named 'agri-chic' so it didn't look or feel like a conservatory, we were

delighted that the planners agreed to the idea. Wanting to put a reception in the Great Barn dated right back to Geoffrey Fraser's plans in the early 1970s, and Don Hanson had drawn up outline plans for Carl in the 1980s. It was so obviously the right place. But how to make it open plan and yet secure? How to achieve a part M compliant staircase to the chapel on the first floor without requiring access through reception? The backs of a great many envelopes were scribbled on before Roger Hands came up with the solution of taking the stairs up through the annexe. And how to get daylight into the chapel? The join with the annexe roof is a masterful sleight of hand if you study the geometry. Replacing the corrugated iron roof with thatch was offered as a major planning gain, and we used the modern Dorset model for better fire safety than traditional thatched roofs. The thatch also promised to keep the building's future occupants warm and cut out the noise of rain on tin roofs, although the ongoing insurance costs have weighed much more heavily than we were originally led to believe. Carl had seen a television programme about the restoration of Windsor Castle after the fire, and set his heart on a green oak timber frame. The rest of us were bemused by the cost, but his persistence paid off as the timbers absolutely make the character of the building.

ABOVE: In the Great Barn February 2000. Jim Blackburn of the Timber Frame Company gesticulating possibilities with Carl and builders.

There were a couple of years when we had to promote the existing building to groups with enthusiasm, while at the same time telling prospective funders how hopelessly derelict and out of date it was and how urgently in need of a complete remodelling. It was a complex project to promote as it had so many facets and touched every aspect of our ministry. We had to plan the construction dates over a year ahead because of the long lead time for summer group bookings. Throughout this time we were energetically raising funds. Sarah was writing appeal letters and closeted in all day design meetings with the architect, builders, thatchers, timber framers, electricians and heating engineers who would be involved with

FAR LEFT: The oak frame components assembled in the yard and craned in to the Great Barn on a very wet week in February 2002.

RIGHT: Roger Page lime plastering the shapely old cob walls in the Pound House quiet room.

the construction. As usual we had a very clear idea of how we wanted the finished building to look and function, and begged, cajoled and jumped up and down to ensure people helped us to achieve it. It was often necessary to apply ingenuity and creativity in the face of mountains of regulations.

Once again Roy Peters and his building team rose to the challenge and it was a delight to watch the building taking shape. The whole compound was fenced off for two years but Sheldon life continued around it with programme events, groups and private retreatants. Lodge guests were treated to a grandstand view of the roof timbering and thatching. Many a sermon was conceived from contemplating the craftsmen at work,

and lots of poems on Richard Skinner's Fun with Words workshops during the 12,000-mile service weeks.

As soon as the builders were out of the Pound House half of the project, Hillary and her team moved in with furniture, light fittings, kitchen equipment and all the other finishing touches. The first guests were the Bath and Wells diocesan senior staff and then a 12,000-mile service week in March 2003. We were all delighted with the results – the space, the quality, the character. However, there was still plenty of work to be done as the interior of the Great Barn and

BELOW: Nine thatchers were employed on the new roof, eight of them under 30, signalling the revival of the craft.

all the landscaping were still to be completed. The workweekers in July 2003 performed the marathon feat of painting the whole of the outside of the building. It was August before the Peters family packed up the portacabin and waved goodbye, and the end of the year before we had made the Great Barn fully operational. Five years and a million pounds – exhausting but worth it. Sheldon just the same but completely different. Jim Cotter, leading a retreat that autumn, declared that Sheldon was now in his 'premier league' of retreat houses. Very soon it was hard to remember the cramped kitchens, the smelly washrooms, the dusty dormitories and the infamous 'chastity room' between them. Sheldon took on a more spacious, welcoming and confident air.

The Pig Pens

We needed a breather to recover from the Courtyard, but it wasn't long before it was the turn of the chalets

to be rebuilt. This time the main ministry needs dictating the design were disabled access, more space for private retreatants and better privacy for couples on programme events. Bed numbers for the larger self-catering groups had to be maintained. Years of worrying about how to achieve good disabled access in an aesthetic way were resolved with the idea of putting a wheelchair-friendly path right round the west side of the site. It proved the most troublesome part of the whole design to implement, but in the end it worked.

After over a decade of partnership on Sheldon projects Roy Peters was

ABOVE: Demolition of the Chalets in December 2005.

LEFT: Roger Page and Adrian Canvin setting out for the new roof timbers on the Pound House in 2003.

unavailable for the dates we needed over the winter of 2005/6. The chalets were the most heavily used accommodation on the whole site so we had to turn the construction round in double quick time during the winter months, and we were reluctant to delay another year. The job was put out to competitive tender and we chose Hindsite, a company less than a year old, for the job. All the usual struggles ensued with a refusal on planning first time round and worries about money and scheduling. It proved expensive to design so many features into such small spaces for the new Pig Pens, but this was essential to make the units flexible to receive so many different types of guests.

BELOW: Setting out part of the wheelchair-friendly path in front of the Pig Pens 2006. The Long Barn under scaffold is having its roof painted.

After the archiepiscopal blessing of the foundations in December 2005 the work progressed apace. By Easter we were ready just in time to welcome the first school groups of the summer term.

Maintenance

It doesn't get any easier pouring heart and soul into creating a new building as near to perfect as possible and then releasing it for everyday use. We just have to take the careless marks on the walls or dents in the woodwork or broken pictures in our stride. On the other (more common and more important side) we glow to see guests enjoying and valuing the spaces we have made for them. We try to run a zero tolerance policy on broken things because people tend to look after more carefully a place that feels loved and cared for. The most annoying things are the small details like pull cords that break irreparably on every design of shaver light we have tried; replacing the seals and handles on shower doors; keeping stocks of 101 different types of light bulbs; toilet roll holder components that break and saucepan bottoms that buckle. In every building we have tried to create plenty of storage space yet there is never enough. Our cleaning team help magnificently in the constant and often thankless task of keeping the whole place clean. It's lovely when people do notice and comment on that, and when people show an insider's understanding of what has gone into creating the space. But then we reckon that one of the hallmarks of good design is precisely that you don't notice it, just enjoy it.

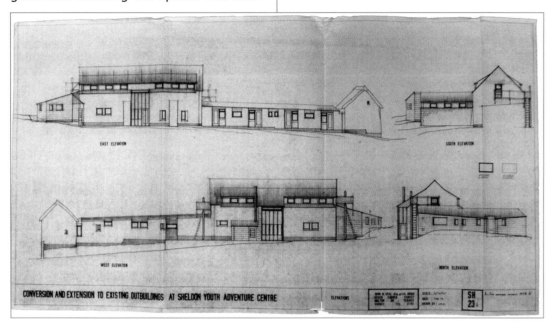

LEFT: Original design drawings, presumably by John Deal, for the 1960s conversion of the Long Barn and pigsties.

Clergy stress

News of the World

After his marriage broke down, the vicar was pilloried across the centre pages of the News of the World for three consecutive weeks. The year was 1973 and the priest in question was a friend of Carl and Sue. It gave them an early insight into the particular, peculiar and sometimes extreme stresses that can go with ministry life. No one else (except perhaps royalty or celebrities) would be treated like that over an intimately personal matter like a marriage breakdown.

During his Church Army training in London Carl was elected senior common room rep. In this role he was involved in some of the pastoral issues surrounding students being removed from college. It involved complex handling of confidential information from different parties, and helping people maintain their dignity at times of turmoil and sometimes shame. Within a few weeks of arriving at Sheldon Carl was asked to provide accommodation for a curate who was being removed from his post after being found in bed with a member of his youth group. Again, it was a formative experience to be alongside someone whose life was suddenly in a big mess awash with practical, emotional and spiritual issues.

BELOW: Home produced 1987 edition of Living with Stress.

Closer to home

As Sheldon developed over the succeeding years, increasing numbers of parish and church youth groups were staying for weekends. It became a familiar pattern for clergy leading the weekends to come in on Sunday afternoon to pay the bill, and find they spent an hour talking to Carl as well. He became concerned by the emerging pattern of isolation, stress and general lack of support experienced by so many clergy he was meeting. Very soon he was talking to people like the Church Army leadership and local bishops about the problem of clergy stress and asking who was going to do what about it. Replies tended to range from 'best not take the lid off that can of worms' to 'problem? what problem?' The latter was often followed within a few weeks by a phone call asking to take someone who 'just needed a break for a little while'. Carl has always been an instinctive listener, but he was concerned that many of the people coming his way needed more specific help than he was able to give at that point. Although Sheldon apparently had lots of beds they were hardly suitable for this sort of ministry. Eventually people like Kenneth Newing (bishop of Plymouth) and Michael Turnbull (chief secretary of the Church Army) started suggesting that if he was so worried about it, maybe he should do something himself.

The financial implications of such a suggestion have been covered in chapter two. However, in spite of the practical obstacles, the vision began to take shape of a safe and supportive place run by a community, and the name Society of Mary and Martha stuck from the early 1980s. We reckoned Jesus might have gone to Bethany when he got stressed and needed space, and the Mary and Martha stories provide lots of food for thought on the themes of prioritising work and prayer. We didn't realise that it would make many people assume it was a wholly female community (probably of Roman Catholic nuns), which is partly why the Sheldon brand has tended to overtake the Mary and Martha one in more recent years. Anyway, we all fight over who gets to open letters addressed to The Mother Superior.

Living with Stress

During her final year of medical training in 1986/7, Sarah had a twelve week period of elective study.

Spying the chance for a sinecure at Sheldon she persuaded psychiatrist Glin Bennet to sign her paperwork saying she would be researching clergy stress. However, dreams of a few months of relaxation evaporated when she started contacting useful people for material and the message repeatedly came back that there was very little written on the subject but people would like to see a copy of

BELOW: Creative headlines from the Sun, Daily Express, Daily Mirror and Independent in August 1987.

ABOVE: Living with Stress.

BELOW: Sarah and Carl at the launch of Living with Stress in the Chapter House at Exeter Cathedral in 1989.

whatever she produced. A period of focused study ensued, at the end of which she rented an Amstrad word processor for a week to type up the results. To her surprise the home produced photocopied Living with Stress booklets started selling, and after 200 had been produced she extended it to a book. Her healthcare underpinnings meant there were a couple of mainstream publishing offers if it could be re-targeted to a general audience. However, she wanted to stick with the focus on the particular needs and stresses of ministry and the book was published by Lutterworth Press in 1989. It was launched in the Chapter House at Exeter Cathedral, and sold a healthy print run of 3,000 copies.

Grabbing the headlines

Although it is only a small proportion of our ministry, it is inevitably vicars and sex that makes headlines. When the charity was launched in the summer of 1987 a conversation on a news-thin bank holiday with a local reporter who turned out to be a stringer for national papers landed us with an array of unexpected headlines. Sarah tried in vain to train Carl to be more judicious in making remarks that could be reported out of context. Sources told us that a local bishop choked on his cornflakes when he opened his holiday newspaper. Anyway, we learned to live by the adage that no publicity is bad publicity, and it certainly got us noticed. A wide range of more sensible press, radio and television interviews followed.

12,000 miles

Long before SMM had a home of its own we started running our own events by hiring Sheldon from the Church Army for a week at a time. The first event was a 12,000-mile service in November 1987. A page of notes from early planning in 1986 calls them Human Service Breaks, and notes 'the need for
- rest - need facilitator, eg massage
- input - affirming individuals, affirming ministry
- food. good food.

n Ecumenical Charity aring for People in Christian Ministry and their Families

- energy release opportunities, physical eg wood chopping
- spiritual framework - daily offices - extended healing service over several days
- feeling of security and relaxation
- feeling secure out of normal environment. avoid anxiety raising.
- briefing before for all those involved
- constant service'

The 12,000-mile service name was intended to convey that this was something you could do on a regular basis as maintenance, instead of waiting for breakdown repairs. Occasionally its mechanical overtones grate, but most people immediately get the idea. We attracted twelve guests each paying the princely sum of £40. Carl roughed out a timetable for the week that has stood for twenty years with only minor amendments. With very little infrastructure at Sheldon, there was a lot of work setting up for such residential events. People were asked to bring their own bed linen if possible, and we bought job lots of fan heaters and hot water bottles to be distributed because there was no central heating in the bedrooms at the time. Chairs and rolls of carpet were carried from one end of the site to the other to try and make the place feel more homely than the basic youth centre it really was. But for all the hard work and lack of creature comforts, we knew that something

really good was happening. We ran two 12,000s the following year, and then three, four or sometimes five every year since. Lots of amazing volunteers helped with cooking, workshops, massage and one-to-one time, contributing a great deal of skill and experience to the fledgling organisation. For the one-to-one work, it has never been easy finding people with the right blend of therapeutic skill, the ability to take everything in their stride, and a willingness to have a full or empty diary for the week. Daphne Norden MMS contacted us looking for an outlet for the skills learned during a year long training in spiritual direction in Chicago. She has continued her regular involvement over fifteen years only taking a break when having to travel extensively on being elected regional leader of her order. Mary Wilson first contacted us offering training workshops in Myers Briggs and Psychosynthesis. We soon discovered

ABOVE: An early promotional leaflet for 12,000s. Before desktop publishing we designed with a combination of calligraphy, letraset and a manual typewriter.

that not only was she a former chair of Relate, but also a talented therapist and experienced clergy trainer and supervisor. She served as a regular lynchpin of 12,000 teams until her death in 2007 and is very sadly missed. Ian Sim, Jim Quin, Richard Skinner and Dot Tesh have also shared this ministry with us, and we continue to keep an ear to the ground for 'wise old birds' to join the team. We have also gathered workshop leaders, again offering a particular intangible blend of activity, reflection and creativity that works in this setting including poetry, art, music, meditation and massage. Nearly a thousand people in ministry have now experienced a 12,000-mile service, and they are still a staple of our programme. They are by far the

most demanding weeks for us as a Community, and we clear our diaries for them accordingly.

Family holiday weeks

Another Mary and Martha classic that emerged early was the clergy family holiday. The idea germinated one autumn after meeting a succession of stressed clergy who had failed to get a decent family break during the summer. Often they had ended up on a wet campsite or staying with relatives for financial reasons, so we thought that a low cost holiday especially for clergy families might be useful. The first one in 1989 included organised outings but we quickly discovered the best formula was to leave the daytime free for families to enjoy independently and then have optional evening activities people could join. For several years the team included Professor Chas Plum and his wife Linnie whose diverse skills included kosher chef, clown and children's entertainer. Catering is a lot easier now we are in the Pound House instead of wet marquees on the lawn or dodging swallows in the Great Barn. Indoor accommodation is still at a premium but it is lovely to see families really relaxing and unwinding together. Clergy children are often singled out as special or different so it is good for them to be able to mix with others in the same boat. We overheard two

BELOW: Liz Bellamy and Peter and Jacky Ward making family holiday week sandwiches in the Pound House cider press in 1994.

youngsters getting to know each other with the question 'Is your Dad a vicar too or is he just normal?' Returning families often say it is the children who insist on booking again, and it's a good place too for families with one or more children with special needs. Our speciality is the designer butty factory where families pick up their packed lunches each morning. Yes, if you want chocolate spread with tomato ketchup that's just fine. Running just two weeks a year we can't compete on play equipment with big family-oriented centres, but in recent years we have invested in a very popular bouncy castle and a splash pool.

Linhay Lodges

Once SMM bought Sheldon in 1991 we were able to start thinking about how we might develop the premises to meet the needs of those coming to us for help in more effective ways. We understood the need and went about trying to meet it, but with little understanding of how much it would change our own lives. As soon as the Linhay lodges were opened we added a whole new dimension to the ministry. As well as self-catering groups and specific programme events we were now welcoming a steady stream of individual guests week in week out. Having focused for several years on the fundraising and construction of the building, it was a bit of a shock to

adapt to the implications of actually running it.

We soon developed a formula for taking lodge bookings. Having an aversion to rationing either by need or ability to pay, we do it simply by releasing some space in advance and keeping some for shorter notice bookings. The latter are more likely to be the emergencies, people signed

off sick or going through a crisis. The method seems to work in both meeting needs usefully and creating a sustainable workload and income stream for Sheldon.

Throughout the construction we referred to 'unit one, unit two' etc

ABOVE: Jan and Lindsey briefing the Linhay lodge teddies (donated by John Wright) before taking up their resident ministry in May 2000.

and puzzled over what to call them. When Carl eventually suggested 'Linhay Lodges' we knew it had the right blend of alliteration and ability to convey the essence of comfort for sojourners stopping over for a short while. Each lodge has a name with various levels of meaning for us. In summary: Thomas because we're big on doubt, David for celtic roots, Clare for women's and monastic ministry, Stephen for martyrdom, and Mary for

appreciation for the resource that makes it all worthwhile, whether they are in floridly visible need, or just want quiet space apart. Once again, it was clear from very early on that we had pinpointed a genuine need and it was a privilege to be able to respond so much more fully. 1,500 guests have stayed in lodges so far, and we hope there will be many more in the years to come. A side-effect of opening the lodges was to change the clientele on 12,000s somewhat. Because they had been the only thing we had to offer, there were more 12,000 guests in the distress throes of a crisis and needing urgent attention. 12,000s these days tend to be a bit steadier partly because we can offer the lodges sooner and for longer, and partly because we are more experienced.

Pig Pens

In 2006 we rebuilt the chalets as the Pig Pens to extend a Linhay Lodge type of resource to more people. We are very aware of shifting patterns of ministry. Our definition of 'ordained and/or full time ministry and/or married to someone who is' has held thus far, but we are conscious of increasing pressures on many lay leaders in churches. We therefore decided that the Pig Pens should be open to everyone and they have been used by a good mix of guests since completion in 2006. Based on

BELOW: Sue Ashby setting up with Sue Price and Jane Seal for a music workshop for a 12,000 mile service in the Pound House cider press in April 1994.

witness to the resurrection. Someone who we showed round the lodges just before completion said they were so nice he reckoned people would take us for a ride. We have never felt that – there has been a strong flavour among clergy of respect and the success of the Linhay Lodges, original suggestions for Pig Pen names included Mini Lodges (descriptive but too difficult to distinguish aurally from Linhay) or Chapel Lodges (geographically accurate but sounded too religious for some). After an intense Community discussion our fondness for historical roots and alliteration won the day again. A few friends raised eyebrows at the choice and one trust wrote a long letter explaining how they couldn't possibly be associated with a project with such a name. However, most guests are tickled by the idea of staying in a Pig Pen.

Programme development

Other things have been tried and refined in developing the programme we run today. Quiet Days have always been popular, but single day workshops have not often worked for us. Putting several shorter events together in one week made things easier to run and Getting to Know God packages morphed into the current Pick and Mix weeks. Things go in and out of fashion, but Myers Briggs, Enneagram and massage courses have all stood the test of time. Mini breaks and quiet weeks came and went but reading weeks currently provide a good framework for people who want unstructured time but with more social contact than a Lodge or Pig Pen allows.

ABOVE: Members of the Consultation Group who were part of the production of Affirmation & Accountability during one of the residential meetings in 2001.

We enjoy inviting leaders to run structured retreats of many different flavours, but the retreat market is a fickle one and it is very hard to predict which will be fully booked a year ahead and which will struggle for numbers. Either way we try very hard not to cancel events because we know how exceedingly annoying it is to have a retreat planned and booked only for it to be cancelled a week before you are due to go away. We get lots of requests from people who want us to book them to run courses and retreats at Sheldon, but we are pretty choosy about who and what gets on the programme. We need to be accountable for the quality of content we promote, and we are the ones carrying the financial risk.

Affirmation & Accountability

One evening in 2001 Carl and Sarah were discussing various recent conversations. They kept hearing the assertion, or at least implication, that clergy who got into stress/trouble shouldn't have been ordained in the first place. Apparently the solution should be better selection to weed out the weaker people before they started. From the high regard we had for many of the guests who passed through Sheldon in difficulties, we did not believe this to be more than very partially true. We started jotting down many of the common reasons people were ending up at Sheldon that seemed to have more to do with

weakness in the organisation than the person. Carl then grandly suggested that a consultation was needed and we would publish a book to share some of our experience back with the wider church. Further jottings came up with a wish list of people we would like to join our consultation, and when every single one said an immediate 'yes' we realised we'd better actually do it. The Jerusalem Trust generously funded three residential gatherings at Sheldon, employment of Barbara Mullett as secretary to the project, plus the cost of the first print run of 1,500. As usual we bit off the mouthful before checking whether we could chew it and it turned into a bigger project than we bargained for. Also as usual, Carl was bored by the time the project was half way through and left Sarah to collate everything and write it up. We were very proud of the end result and published Affirmation and Accountability in 2002. The first copies were distributed at the biannual three day conference of the Anglican Association of Pastoral Care and Counsellors at Launde Abbey where Sarah was the keynote speaker. Bishop Peter Selby was the conference facilitator and pronounced that A&A would be a success because 'it is beautiful, it has a sense of humour, and it does not have Archbishops' Council on the cover'. We believe it has been a success in a quiet and perhaps subversive way, with 4,000 copies

BELOW: Affirmation and Accountability

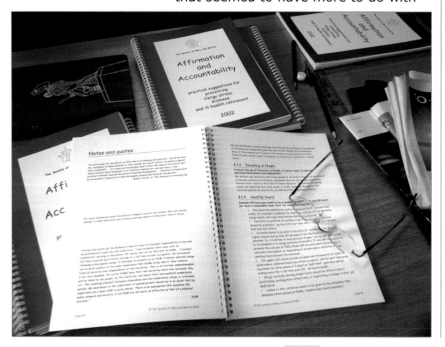

in circulation, discussed by diocesan senior staff and clergy chapters all over the country. In order to avoid the pitfalls of over-generalisation we restricted the focus to the anglican church of England and Wales. We were delighted that many churches overseas and in different denominations also took it up enthusiastically to translate as appropriate to their own situations. Many of the issues we raised in 2002 have proved prescient and the manual has so far stood the test of time. We wish we had had sufficient time and money to do some sort of follow up such as questionnaires or a web-based discussion board. However, as we were still in the thick of building the Courtyard we decided we simply had to give birth to our baby and let it go out and fend for itself. We received dozens of invitations to speak, but with just a small home team to deal with the demands of running a residential resource we turned them all down. If we had done our job well enough the manual would serve as a workbook that people could use in their own way. Several dioceses set up working parties specifically to look at how recommendations might be implemented locally. We didn't receive any formal feedback, but we know for instance that our checklist of recommendations on handling clergy off sick was adopted wholesale in some dioceses. It would be nice to know about any implementation experience.

Five years on A&A unexpectedly gained a second lease of life with a flurry of sales, and it is now available as an e-book downloaded from our website.

Keeping Mum

Confidentiality is a core value of our ministry, and we have considered its outworkings very carefully. The world of the church is a very small one, and people can be identified from fairly slender details so we talk very sparingly and only in strictly general terms about those who come here. We are aware of the risk that places like Sheldon can become gossip junctions but maybe we sometimes fall into the opposite trap of being too taciturn. It certainly doesn't do our fundraising

ABOVE: Adoramus singing Advent Music in the Long Barn in 1994. We try to make sure there are plenty of opportunities to 'dip in' to Sheldon.

and publicity profile any good. We liaise occasionally with medical practitioners under formal consent arrangements. We sometimes have an initial telephone call from church leaders who want to recommend and/or pay for someone to come here, but they can't 'send' anyone, and we don't talk further once the person themselves has made contact.

Implementation of confidentiality is about giving people privacy and space. On an early 12,000 we discovered guests in the library looking each other up in Crockfords (yes really) so after that we stuck to Christian names only in all our day to day dealings around Sheldon. The 'no clergy shop talk' part of the house rules can be immensely challenging because the habitual initial connection points between strangers are 'what do you do?' and 'where do you come from?'. Both questions can unwittingly be painfully intrusive to people here for respite from either or both, so we try, with varying degrees of success, to bypass them straight to more neutral topics of conversation. Our experience has led us to take the rule very seriously but some guests treated it as a gimmick to be ignored, so in 2003 we introduced a line on the booking form for people to sign agreement to abide by the house rules. These occasionally get waved at offenders, and we designed a tactful yellow card to help some of those who don't realise they are transgressing.

Our house rules were given a national airing when vicar Janet Fisher from radio four's The Archers visited Sheldon in 2002. Fans will remember she was going through a stressful time struggling not to follow her heart and get involved with the unhappily married Tim Hathaway. Although SMM wasn't mentioned by name our ministry was clearly recognisable and we received many phone calls and emails from excited friends.

Strict confidentiality is occasionally vital for people who are being pursued by the press or by someone dangerous. Our staff are trained never to disclose who is staying at Sheldon, even inadvertently, to avoid being tricked by someone devious who is trying to get information. This can be annoyingly cumbersome for people genuinely needing to make contact, but for the occasional guest it is vital.

Hospitality

Many of those who cross our threshold are tired, anxious, stressed or depressed. Most people in ministry live on the job, so they may be coming to Sheldon as a refuge when people in other walks of life might prefer to retreat to the security of their own home. We have tried to understand this across all aspects of the hospitality we offer. It might be Hillary's choice of restful furnishings or tasty food for a stocked larder; Carl's laying out a new garden or a setting out a timetable; Sarah's design of booking information or training of reception staff; Jan's gentle massage or punctual meals; Sue's hosting at the bar or the shop. One of the nicest, and quite regular, feedback comments is 'you've thought of everything'. We try to. There is a Sheldon Community passion for attention to detail at all levels. We close Sheldon for Community holidays a couple of times a year and have house sitters to look after the place. One prospective house sitter asked if it wouldn't be better to keep Sheldon open 'and let those who normally do the jobs carry on as usual'. Well actually, that would be us - and we need a holiday.

Resources

Although some guests simply do their own thing, many take advantage of additional resources. If things look quite complicated, longer stay Lodge guests will sometimes have an initial session with both Carl and Sarah to sort out a strategy for their visit.

A great deal of the therapeutic work is done simply by letting the place do its thing in lowering arousal levels, creating space for decent sleep, eating properly and pacing the day. Enjoying the grounds is a good way to get exercise to help with sleep and mood, and to focus the attention away from negative ruminations. Sometimes

ABOVE: A Myers Briggs workshop in the Long Barn led by Christine Clarke and Rosemary Dawn Watling in 1995. The chairs had many generations of green covers sewn at Sheldon.

ABOVE: Hillary introducing school children to the donkeys in 1992.

bereavement, sexuality, legal or disciplinary proceedings, etc. We have learned to be pretty much unshockable and by now we really have seen most of it all before.

Twenty years ago it was common for Christians to feel quite shamed and isolated by a diagnosis of depression. The stigma has reduced but the prevalence has increased so quick and effective talking treatments are in demand. Massage was considered 'new age' and extremely suspect when we first offered it back in the 1980s. It is now much more widely accepted and many people have their first ever massage at Sheldon because they feel safe enough to try something new.

We know that the Sanctuary and the Community's daily offices can be important resources in re-connecting with a God who has disappeared or let people down. We try to be aware and reflective as journey companions and keep a light touch in supporting that most delicate of relationships. Falling out with God is a very big deal for religious professionals and layered with many flavours of guilt and self-blame. Carl believes especially in the value of paying deep attention to people's unique stories and helping them shape the next stage of their journeys. We don't pray with people, but we regularly pray for them. We don't consider ourselves to be 'Christian

all this comes naturally to people when they are given the resources, but those who are highly stressed or in combative mode sometimes need explicit help to settle. This might be through a massage from Jan, or playing with the art box. Sarah likes tecchie gadgets and has accumulated a Capnograph and a Resperate for helping people to calm their breathing, plus various recording equipment for making personalised relaxation tapes. People are generally much quicker to gain a productive fresh perspective on whatever crisis they are facing when the basics are attended to first rather than rushing straight in with a focus on the problems. Those problems might relate to anything like work overload, poor health, being bullied, relationship stress or disaster, family issues, counsellors' but people who share a common faith and come equipped to support body, mind and soul.

If it sounds too low-key and simple, we like it to look that way on the surface, although of course we work carefully and think very hard about what we do with each individual. Along the way we do seem to have built up some genuine and rather unique expertise in creating first class restorative space for people in ministry who hit a rough patch.

Our aim always is to welcome people as fellow-travellers with dignity and respect. It is our hope and prayer that a sojourn at Sheldon will strengthen and equip guests for the journey ahead. Some we meet only once, others find an oasis to which they return regularly.

Hosting groups

Before any of our programme and private retreat resources began, and still interwoven with them today, are the self-catering groups. A few have been regulars for over thirty years including Roger Attwood bringing PHAB groups from London complete with wheelchairs and food mountains,

ABOVE: A camp exercise book from Chudleigh primary school in 2005 complete with a fat pigeon.

LEFT: Tent city on the Pound House lawn with Stoke Canon school in 1993. We all enjoyed the aroma of eggy bread being cooked for breakfast on their camp fire.

and John Robbins bringing outward bound groups from Sussex complete with canoes and lycra. In the 1970s Devon County Council had a block booking and the place hosted lots of school groups. Sarah first came to Sheldon aged eleven in 1974 when she helped milk goats in the Linhay, got lost orienteering in the copse, and did a project on mining in the local area. Concerns over Sheldon's fire safety precautions (almost certainly unfounded) led to termination of the county's involvement and a diversification of the group bookings. Various local parishes made Sheldon the venue for their annual parish retreat/holiday. Many people who

grew up as members of the parish of Central Exeter remember halcyon weekends here as children. Although we have specialised in providing for a more adult clientele in recent years, we know that Sheldon still has important things to offer young visitors which is why we make sure that buildings and grounds are user-friendly for all ages: robustly built so things aren't easily broken, and bedrooms suitable for packing in larger numbers when necessary. For many seven year olds from Chudleigh school, Sheldon is their first ever night away from home. Children have been making the coach journey from St Nicolas' School, Newbury for their leavers' field trip for so many years it has become the eagerly anticipated stuff of school legend. Teachers from special schools have always especially appreciated the round the clock availability of a resident Community. There is a greater risk of unexpected happenings when taking learning disabled youngsters away as part of their journey to greater self-reliance. More recently Sheldon has enjoyed the sticky-fingered explorations of a dozen babies with their teenage mums from Bristol on a training event, and the annual weekend of the Teign Valley Fun Club. Student Christian unions, Alpha groups, church holidays, parish retreats, extended family celebrations, drama, study, walking, yoga, meditation, leadership

BELOW: Bible study for students from Bath Spa in the Long Barn in 2003.

training – the faces and group names change, but we continue to welcome a very rich variety of groups doing their own catering, running their own programme.

There must be tens of thousands of people who have stayed here over the years, but where does this side of Sheldon now fit with our core commitment to care for people in Christian ministry? At the mundane level it is a practical way of sharing the overheads and making a sustainable lifestyle for the Community. The costs of running the buildings and grounds are shared between the intensive work of our specialist ministry and groups who make good use of the premises while contributing financially and needing less attention from us. We are also aware of another theme. It might have been easy for SMM to have a reputation as somewhere that was only for people in crisis. A funny farm for cracked up clergy. It doesn't take much imagination to see the stigma that would be attached to needing help from such a place. The ordinariness of Sheldon, the fact that so many people come here for such ordinary reasons, really helps to keep the hurdles low for those who are in crisis but don't find it

LEFT: Jan and Hillary at the opening of the Fat Pigeon bar in the Loose Box in July 2004. We love creating good space for people to be.

easy to ask for help. Issues of stigma and reputation will always be subtle and challenging. Even with all our efforts in this direction, it was pretty obvious that no-one wanted to be seen talking to Carl when he attended a clergy reception at the bishop's palace. We welcome people wanting ordinary time out, we welcome people struggling at the limits of their ability to cope. The mix itself is important and seems to benefit both.

Chapels and prayers

Anciently a small chapel

The rector of Doddiscombsleigh recorded in the 1720 census that there was a chapel at Sheldon used by the catholic family living there. White's 'Devon' in 1850 records that 'there was anciently a small chapel at Sheldon'. According to the Listing of Buildings of Special Architectural or Historic Interest, it was probably built in the late fifteenth century 'a small single cell building, rectangular in plan, on an east/west axis. Remarkable three bay late C15 unceiled wagon roof with

BELOW and RIGHT: 1960s restoration of the Chapel in progress.

moulded ribs; wall plates carved with a bold beaded ribbon.' We believe that the wooden panels lining the walls were sold to America in the 1930s. The building adjoined the pigsties, and was used as a store for the pig feed. A door was knocked through the north wall to give easier access.

In the late 1960s the chapel was renovated under the direction of John Deal and Geoffrey Fraser. As an architect training students at Kingston upon Thames, John was able to draw on a pool of willing hands to help with the project. The roof was dismantled and restored, but when it came to putting it back it didn't fit properly. Some very twentieth century telegraph poles came to the rescue as a wall plate – Geoffrey had bought a job lot of poles and they came in handy all

over the place. Until Carl arrived the chapel was used as a quiet space but had no cross or anything to designate it as a Christian place of worship, although he believes there were occasional eucharists celebrated there by the Harvesters.

Within days of arriving Carl was in the chapel with his usual habit of saying morning and evening prayer (series three in those days). It was at the time when Dutch elm disease was rife and elm trees had to be removed. In the back garden was an elm tree sucker, and he cut that, peeled it, tied it with a bit of string and hung it on the wall. The simple cross and the striking, almost human, shadow it cast on the uneven cob wall behind, was later incorporated into the Sheldon logo.

LEFT : Pauline Mortimer's painting of Community prayers in the medieval chapel full of Easter flowers – mid 1980s.

BELOW: Reassembling chapel roof trusses in the late 1960s.

The original was found to be full of woodworm after nearly twenty years, and was replaced with one similar, this time made of willow.

When the Church Army bought Sheldon in 1977 various furnishings were available also. Carl turned down Geoffrey's offer of the table serving as

Have you looked at the roof of the chapel? Count the trusses, you will find there are eleven, the last (the twelfth) on to the west wall is missing and the thatch battens run into the cob. This is common on pre-reformation buildings, say 1450-1530. Twelve disciples less Judas, eleven. Look again and miss out in your mind the later repairs, you should find no iron. Iron nails were used to hang Christ to the Cross. Now look at the rib vaults, you will see that there are some remaining, this shows that at one time the soffit was plastered, the lathing being tied to the ribs and divided into panels. These would have been painted probably blue (the celestial firmament) the ribs picked out in red/blue or gold. Now look down to the wall plate, you will see ears of corn cut into the plate. Normally there are six ears (seven years of plenty, so don't tempt fortune) the number again should be in a multiple of seven less one (normally). The east wall would have been painted over with a depiction of the tree of life (or similar). I think this was built by a devout Catholic, at ease with his God, making a good living off the land, maybe a minor Lord. It is unusual to see what was once so common place relatively unmolested. Imagine your self back say 1510 ish, incense burning together with the sanctuary lamp, a small altar with flowers candles and cross, heavily painted walls and soffit, small window with light streaming in picking out the smoke. The floor strewn with reeds. The Lord's wife at her morning prayers with her children and a visiting priest or monk from a local Abbey. Outside the bustle of a busy working farm, the smell of horses and cattle. The young son returning from hunting with a hawk and hounds, him on horse back his retainer on foot. Smoke from the house kitchens, all surrounded by a stockade. Mud and stuff under foot, clothing homespun...
Anthony Mealing Dip ARCH, RIBA, AABC. MaPS Chartered Architect.

RIGHT: In the Long
Barn after Easter
Midnight Eucharist
1987. Including Kenneth
Newing, Sam Davies,
Gibson Pattison, John
Wensley, Suzanne
Reilley, Wendy
Thompson and Sybil
Button.

an altar in chapel because its rickety legs and unstable leaves were nothing but a nuisance. Geoffrey had great delight in telling Carl he had sold it for £600 – a princely sum. Carl preferred the sturdy tables at the Teign House Inn just down the road and bought one for £12. Sue's Dad made the cupboard and shelves on the back wall that for many years held service books, candles and other liturgical bits and pieces.

Because of the loss of civic records in the second world war nobody was able to find out what had been the original dedication of the chapel. The Sheldon Family chose Christ the Servant as a symbol of their desire to be of service to those who came to Sheldon. A statue was commissioned from a sculptor in Oxford but by the time it arrived in 1982, most of those who had commissioned it had left and Carl was left to find £300 to foot the bill. The dedication was carried out by Kenneth

RIGHT: Medieval chapel full of visiting angels Christmas 1990.

Newing. Most of the service took place in a marquee as the chapel is so small.

Ernie Townsend built perimeter seating around 1980, and had a cross of nails made in Brighton which he placed above the door. Carl and Sarah built the round construction in the corner to put the statue on and create somewhere for candles. It would have been better with a more in depth understanding of plumb line and spirit level. The carved head of Christ came from Jack Money in Brighton. Kate Gardner made the ceramic candle holders and the framed textile that hung in the alcove (blocked up pigsty doorway) for many years.

The chapel continued in regular use for morning and evening prayer every weekday as part of the rhythm of life of the Sheldon Family and then

Community. At Easter it was filled to bursting with flowers. One year Kenneth Newing got too enthusiastic with the incense in the tiny space and the door had to be opened wide and Jenny Hanson laid out on the bench seating to recover. Cardboard cut out angels assembled all round the walls during Advent. For a few years the Sheldon Community made its own crib figures from clay or playdough. The experiment ground to halt when Hillary's dog ate two (very salty) shepherds and we got fed up with kind enquirers asking whether our crib had been made by the local primary school children.

With a very limited electricity supply, the chapel was always cold. The colder the weather the shorter our prayers. A generous collection in memory of Michael Lillingston-Price meant we were able to put in some small wall-mounted heaters, and new lights that could be faded up and down. In 2005 we decided it was time to rethink the chapel to make it a warmer and more accessible place for private prayer for the increasing number of people making retreats at Sheldon. With underfloor heating planned for the Pig Pens, we could extend it to the chapel and get everything sorted out together. In fact the Pig Pens project was proving complicated to manage, and we belatedly realised planning permission was needed to

LEFT: The Shepherd's Sanctuary in the Linhay looking out onto the medieval chapel.

put the heating in the chapel, so it was delayed until 2007. The work was all planned and we arranged a eucharist as the final act of worship before pulling out all the interior fittings. With customary itchy fingers Carl had already pulled up all the floor tiles before the service, and within two hours afterwards he and Simon were standing, perspiring, in a large pile of rubble. Carl was determined to knock apart the 'wedding cake' structure in the corner personally as he had built it a quarter of a century previously. It appeared to have been built more like

a bomb shelter than a candle-holder. Simon teased him that he should recite 'I must not over-engineer' with every swing of the sledgehammer. Soon the chapel was re-opened with a subtle hint of a cross in the newly tiled and warmed floor, and a beautiful oak bench along the west wall designed by Adrian Canvin. We hope it will continue as a good place for prayer for many years.

Shepherd's Sanctuary

When we built the Linhay in 1997 we felt strongly that there should be a private prayer space for those seeking sanctuary here. It is a tiny space with slit windows to match the medieval chapel. During construction it was a constant battle to keep the space clear of all the useful things builders like somewhere to put, such as pipes and header tanks and fuse boxes.

It is called the Shepherd's Sanctuary because with the door at the top of an outside stair, you step out and look across to the sheep field. Carl and Hillary bought a shepherd's crook (technically a market stick) at Mole Valley Farmers and made it into a cross for the wall. Sarah found an aumbry, reputedly from a church in India, at an antiques shop on Exeter quay and Adrian Canvin gave it a top to make a diminutive altar table. The cushioned recess was nicknamed the bus stop – somewhere to wait for God. Bishop Ted soon took up residence. He was a well-patched teddy with a pectoral cross made from olive wood from the Holy Land, given by Janice Lamb. A surprise gift of £20,000 towards construction came from the Rank Foundation in memory of one of our patrons, Donald English. We later heard that the wife of a trustee had met the wife of a vicar who had been put back together at Sheldon

conscious that being in the round made visitors quite exposed, especially if they came in late. When we started the plans for the Courtyard, we made the big decision to allocate almost all the upstairs of the Great Barn as a chapel. We could have had more bedrooms, more offices, etc, but opted for God space at the heart of the new development. Originally Carl wanted a round window in the end wall but the logistics of the oak frame and the pitch of the thatched roof did not allow it so we opted for two slit windows to match the medieval chapel and the sanctuary. They make a small but significant connection between the chapel and the outside world. One of the fundraising

LEFT and BELOW:
The medieval chapel soon after the 1960s restoration.

and had good reports of the place. We can't mention names because we don't know them, but we were grateful for the value of good gossiping about the Sheldon ministry. We know the sanctuary is well used from the lights that often shine out in the evening, and the rate at which matches, candles and tissues get used.

Mary, Martha and Lazarus

As more guests were staying at Sheldon and wanting to join Community prayers, it was becoming increasingly difficult to fit into the medieval chapel. We were also very schemes was for people to buy an oak peg that would hold the building together, and Carl wrote hundreds of names on pegs. The big purlin behind the altar was funded in memory of John Smith. Simon Lee fashioned a cross from old oak beams from the Farmhouse. It is so heavy it has to be held securely in place by a bolt and farm gate-hook. Candlesticks and snuffers were made by Maurice Price, and the Red Madonna icon was sold in aid of the North Devon Children's Hospice. We imagined that Community daily offices would alternate between the old and new chapels. However, it was immediately obvious that more people felt able to join us when they could just slip in anonymously at the back and not even pick up a book if they didn't want to, and so we stayed in the new. Mary, Martha and Lazarus seemed the obvious dedication for the new chapel, but because that is a bit of a mouthful we usually refer to it simply as the upstairs chapel. As well as daily prayers, it hosts special events like Advent Music, Friday Fringe, Community Re-dedication, Candlemas, New Year's Eve, visiting groups, and our own retreats. We hope that the simple solid green oak beams will stand for as long as those of the medieval chapel we have inherited.

Pray as you can

It's not uncommon for guests to say they find our daily prayers rather dull, sparse or boring. It's a fair criticism, but one we find painful even so. It's not easy for a small group to maintain a faithfully regular pattern week in week out for decades. We see that faithfulness of presence and intercession as an important witness. Sometimes the repetition and simplicity is a weakness, sometimes it is a strength, but it is always there. We generally stick to basically anglican patterns of canticles and readings, starting and signing off the working day with space that is set apart for God. Sometimes we're bored, sometimes we're preoccupied, but most of the time we're there. It's

BELOW: New Year's Eve Eucharist 2002 in the Long Barn with Mary Weatherley.

A few prayer times have always been kept private to the Community. Since the mid 1990s we have held Community vigils a week before Easter and before the summer Community re-dedication. We currently have a monthly 9pm prayer meeting, and weekly 9pm compline during lent and advent. They are important times for sharing prayer needs with each other as well as being quiet together.

As for many other Christians, changing patterns of clergy deployment have shifted our patterns of eucharistic

LEFT: Simon Lee hanging the cross of old oak on the green oak collar of the upstairs chapel in 2004.

nothing special, we can't sing so we don't, and it's fairly short. Those who join us are not wowed by creative liturgy, but we know that many, many people value the dependable routine of the prayers of the community. Since 1987 we have maintained a regular prayer cycle of Friends of Mary and Martha, we pray for guests, we pray for people in ministry, and we pray for people in special need. To maintain privacy and confidentiality we only use Christian names on our prayer lists and sometimes even pseudonyms. God knows.

LEFT: Richard Hawkins at the blessing of the Sanctuary late on Easter eve 1999.

ABOVE: Richard Hawkins, with Mary Weatherley and William Parker, blessing the prayer meadow in the barn field July 2004.

celebration at Sheldon. In the early 1980s there was a regular Wednesday 8am eucharist with Gibson Pattison, rector of Dunsford. As valley parishes amalgamated it was no longer reasonable to ask someone to make such a regular commitment to a small group of people. We made an early decision that we would not ask guests to preside (although many offer) as we felt it blurred necessary role boundaries. Derek Atkinson was chaplain to the Community in the early 1990s, and during the years Mary Weatherley was living alongside the Community she presided once a fortnight. Other local Friends or resident volunteer clergy kindly pitch in when invited for midweek celebrations. Community Feasts evolved out of eucharists to celebrate special occasions such as Candlemas to which we invited a few immediate friends, and then added a meal and invited all Friends of SMM in the area.

Judith Ware was living alongside the Community when we hit a periodic rocky patch. She commented that most other communities she knew called more prayer meetings when things were going badly while we cancelled chapel. It doesn't happen often, but occasionally it has been just too hard even to pray together. It can be a difficult line between being honest about what we're feeling and opting out, and keeping the show on the road regardless. We have found that the routine can sometimes help to hold us through the bumpier rides.

Laying aside

Stephen Colver designed a small brown square card with the Sheldon dove logo and the following prayer

Here may you lay aside
burdens borne for
self and others
May this place be to you
a vessel of love
Wherefrom you may draw
Rest, Silence, Healing, Vision

And may the Creator's love
warmly glow
from all that you see
Welcome

Each card had the guest's name written on and left by their bed. Later the prayer was also used on welcome leaflets and in the front of the folders in Lodges and Pig Pens. It has stood the test of time.

Transition and continuity

We mark a great many transitions with some sort of liturgy, especially when people arrive or leave, and buildings are gutted or demolished, commissioned or re-ordered. We light candles, say prayers, burn incense and sprinkle holy water. During workparties we will often gather for prayers at different places around the site,

whether that be the opening of the mediterranean garden, night prayers in each of the chalets as they were gutted or the lodges as they were being built. Three Easter eucharists were held in the Great Barn; before the Courtyard development, half way through, and with the new chapel boarded out but not yet completed. We have a strong sense of our built and natural spaces being inhabited through prayer and presence and try to find simple and effective ways to express this. Our annual Candlemas service involves a candlelit procession and prayers around the site.

Each July we have a simple service of re-dedication for our ministry for the year ahead. The current service has been used in roughly the same format since 1999 with a reading from Philippians and one from Henri Nouwen, a symbolic pouring of water, sharing and returning it to source, and a communal confession and absolution. We have not yet got very far with actually writing down a Community Rule of Life, but the service incorporates the core themes of servanthood, stewardship and stability that we seek to develop in our individual and common life.

ABOVE: Community candles around the Paschal candle in the upstairs chapel after Community rededication in 2007.

LEFT: The Great Barn set up for the Easter Eucharist in 2001 as part of the prayerful preparation for the Courtyard development.

Events and celebrations

Just to prove we can make an 'event' out of almost anything:

RIGHT: Raising the flag for the Queen's birthday on a wet April day, including Steve Murphy, Tez Hastings and Paul Welch.

RIGHT: Hillary opening the newly tarmaced drive during workweek in July 1999.

Anyone who spends time at Sheldon knows that Carl is always on the lookout to spice up life with a party, a celebration, an occasion of any sort. According to his diary, the first occasion at Sheldon was when he and Sue invited the Sheldon management committee to supper on Oct 7th 1976 to get to know people better – apparently plenty of alcohol flowed.

Fireworks

The first Sheldon bonfire night was run in 1976 for Plymstock youth group who were in residence for the weekend. The barbecue was laid on by curate David Chance, and the fireworks by Carl. With Lewes Bonfire in his blood, Carl continued letting off fireworks most years until Margaret Thatcher legislated small time operators out of existence. The house specialities were

big shells (fired from six inch steel mortar tubes made by Ken Pim) and set piece tableaux with lance work ahead of their time. We can remember a galactic theme with spaceship and daleks, two windmills (Jim Pilkington fell off a ladder getting the sails to turn), two big battle ships, and St George complete with castle and fire-breathing dragon. The biggest night started late because cars were queuing down to the Teign House Inn. Philip Johanson (Carl's head of department at CA HQ) was allocated entrance gate duties, and queried where all the income was appearing in the accounts. It wasn't (and nor was the expenditure), but the recycled money supported Andy Leigh for his year at Sheldon. Fireworks might be accompanied by Roland Saffin lamb roasts, Radio Sheldon broadcasts, or hot soup from the roadshow bus.

Mortars were fired out of Ed Brook's metal silage trailer for extra sound effects. One year the bus got stuck in the camping field and stayed there until it could be ignominiously towed out the following spring. When the National Trust at Killerton celebrated 300 years of William and Mary, Carl was the only local person they could find who could create a special lancework motif. We borrowed £2,000 from Frank Firkin to fund the purchase of fireworks which were duly let off to orchestral accompaniment in Killerton's parkland.

In 1977 the then trustees of Sheldon were trying to raise £40,000 to buy out Geoffrey Fraser. On 14th April an Any Questions evening was held in Exeter Guildhall to launch the first Sheldon appeal. On the panel were David Jacobs, Wilf Westall (Bishop of Crediton and a regular on Radio four's Any Questions), Margaret Branch (Guide Commissioner for Exeter and still a Friend), Brian Stephenson

(Professor of Geography at Exeter University), and Carl (expert on Sheldon.) Unfortunately it only raised £4,000, but the evening was good fun.

At 9pm on 6th June 1977 Carl lit a beacon in the camping field for the queen's silver jubilee. The day stands out in Carl's memory as the day an agitated Church Army officer rushed into his office having caught sight of a female member of staff stark naked, and demanding to know what was going to be done.

27th May 1978 was a very hot sunny day with a medieval fayre held at Sheldon. Stalls, crafts, beekeeping, thatching, jousting, ballista battle and birds of prey. Jerry Horsman (Sarah's

LEFT: HMS Ark off to be blown up in 1987.

BELOW: St George and the dragon with Phil Searle, Steve Thompson, Carl, Chris Cockman.

ABOVE: Bertha having a polish from Steve Thompson.

BELOW: domestic life on board including Paul Welch and Kate Elkins.

RIGHT: Carl and Sarah in the DevonAir studio ~ 1990.

Dad) sheared Pip Bug's bony Jacob sheep for an appreciative audience of children squeaking 'Ooh look Mummy, he's cut it again – more blood'. The following day Simon Lee was baptised at Dunsford Church, with a family party at Sheldon afterwards.

Roadshow and mission

The Church Army Roadshow ran from 1981 to 1988. A team toured with music and drama sketches to shows and resorts locally and as far afield as London, Darlington, York, Brighton and Skegness. A three ton lorry was converted to open out into a stage, and was painted up in an unsubtle livery of purple, yellow and blue. Living quarters were very cramped in a caravan and the lorry cab, so the following year a double decker bus was added to the fleet and kitted out with dormitories upstairs, kitchen downstairs, and a large awning. Mike Gardner took the bus for a test drive and realised along the winding road to Moretonhampstead that he had better turn round before he got to Dartmoor. As Mike executed the manoeuvre in a lay-by overlooking a perilous drop down the Teign Gorge, a four year old Simon Lee was heard to breathe 'boogger me' as he peered out from the top deck window. We're not sure if anyone got converted as a result of our evangelistic endeavours, but there were plenty of adventures with low bridges, one way streets

and muddy fields. To assist with the latter we bought thirty army sand ladders from Roger Jamison's yard on the Sheldon lane. They have served many uses at Sheldon over the years, and we eventually sold two of them for the price of the entire job lot to a chap who needed them as must-have accessories for his armoured personnel carrier.

Through the 1970s and '80s Carl led various parish missions (All Saints Clevedon, St Paul's Tiverton, St John's Lewes), plus beach missions at Dawlish and Torquay and children's clubs at Burnthouse Lane, St Thomas's, and Heavitree, all in Exeter.

Local radio

In 1987 John Murch mentioned that the post of religious adviser to DevonAir radio was currently vacant. Carl expressed an interest to the bishop and was duly appointed. He much enjoyed presenting the weekly religious programme for several years,

first a half hour show at 7.30am on Sunday mornings, then 9-10pm Sunday evenings, with longer specials on Christmas Day. Tez Hastings and Chris Cockman worked the technicals. Sarah originally came along to make tea and let guests in, and eventually joined Carl behind the microphone. Lots of local people came in to the studio to be interviewed live on air. Guests who had led sheltered lives were occasionally disconcerted when the glamorous Caroline Jane appeared in the studio towards the end of the show, and then started broadcasting in rich bass tones as Glen Richards. Her fascinating story is told in A Tale of Two Sexes, kindly donated to our library. Carl was very chuffed to record a telephone interview with Cliff Richard in December 1990 which was broadcast when Saviour's Day hit number one in the charts a couple of weeks later. Carl was famous for running competitions where he gave away the answer in the question as in 'What kind of dove, I mean bird, fetched a leaf to Noah in the Ark?' Lots of books were sent to be reviewed. We can't remember ever actually reviewing a book on air, but the collection made a great start for the Sheldon library in 1993.

Inaugural Eucharist

The first Society of Mary and Martha event was the Inaugural Eucharist held

in a marquee at Sheldon in July 1987. Kenneth Newing celebrated and John Perry preached. A eucharist on the Saturday nearest the feast of Mary, Martha and Lazarus became an annual event. We always read the Mary and Martha reading from Luke's gospel and we've heard a good variety of sermons on the theme over the years. In 1992 we decamped up to Doddiscombsleigh church because the marquee had been flooded out. Whatever the occasion, we always did our best to get some publicity out of it. After SMM bought Sheldon, the event was often combined with a blessing or the opening of one project or another. In July 1993 Rosemary Howell opened the Woodshed, in 1997 Roger Royle and Richard Hawkins cut our 10th birthday

ABOVE: Inaugural Eucharist July 1987.

BELOW: Proud parents at Simon Lee's baptism.

ABOVE: Annual Eucharist in the theatre in 1992.

a We are Staying party to celebrate the completion of the purchase of Sheldon from the Church Army. We cut a huge great cardboard key which everyone held for a photo-op in the gateway. After our difficult experiences of local hostility it was a delight that so many local people supported the purchase and wanted to celebrate with us. It had been a very tense and anxious five months of fund-raising and conveyancing and it was hard to believe that Sheldon was now independently owned by SMM – the start of a new era.

Sheldon weddings

Two Sheldon marriages were celebrated in 1996. Sarah Lee married Gary Bovey on 27th July in the theatre. Phil Searle conducted the ceremony, Sarah H made the wedding dress, and Hillary laid on the catering. A disco by Phil Hutchins and Carl was held in the Animal Barn in the evening. On the 26th August,

cake, in 2004 Richard Hawkins blessed the Prayer Meadow, and in 2005 we sang Bless to us this Land written by Sue Ashby as we processed up to the Spanishlake fields.

The TV cameras followed Sir Harry Secombe to Sheldon in 1990 to film an edition of Highways. It was a formidable team including Sir Harry's management and the TV crew. Sir Harry himself was incredibly friendly, walking straight up, shaking Carl's hand and taking him off for a walk through the woods, talking nineteen to the dozen. He later became a patron of SMM.

RIGHT: Harry Secombe being filmed with Carl by the celtic huts in the copse.

One of our happiest celebrations was on 31st August 1991 when we threw

Phil Searle married Claire Collins on a very wet day in the marquee. Carl looked after Phil's teddy to make sure he got a good view of the rainbow proceedings conducted by Ross Bell. The ultra-inclusive reception in the barn reflected the diversity of the kingdom of heaven, followed by a well-oiled ceilidh.

Buildings works celebrations

The building of the Linhay was a big project, and as usual construction work was started while there was still lots of money to be raised. We invited those already involved with the project, plus potential funders, to a start of works ceremony. The Earl of Morley laid the foundation stone, Richard Eyre, dean of Exeter, said prayers and Hillary laid on a slap up lunch in the conservatory. Photos of the day were a bit limited as the photographer we had hired was more interested in the girl he brought with him than in our proceedings. When the roof was on we had an Easter Monday topping out ceremony when Hewlett Thompson, bishop of Exeter mounted the scaffolding to hammer in the symbolic final nail. With two fingers strapped up in a finger stall people joked that he had been practising beforehand. We assembled under a clear sky, but from the scaffold a large dark cloud could be seen appearing on the horizon. By the time we reached the appointed hour for the ceremony it was not just raining but throwing down huge bouncing hailstones. We had

ABOVE: Christopher Airy opening the Conservatory in 1996.

LEFT: Sarah Lee on her way to the wedding ceremony in the theatre with the father of the bride.

LEFT: The animal barn lit up for Phil and Claire's wedding ceilidh.

better luck with the weather for the blessing and dedication of the Linhay in July 1999. A traditional haywagon pulled by a carthorse was deemed a suitably picturesque centrepiece for the occasion. After the annual eucharist in the theatre, all those who were robed, including Michael Mayne (celebrant) and Michael Turnbull (preacher) clambered up into the wagon, sat down on straw bales, and were conveyed in style up through the yard. Apparently the non-existent suspension gave all their bones a good shaking. Bishop Hewlett gave the blessing of the Linhay from the wagon. We didn't realise until they reached the Long Barn that a horse and cart has such a big turning circle and no brakes, so manoeuvring in a limited space was a delicate

THIS PAGE: Linhay ceremonies: Foundation stone with Lord Morley and Roy Peters. Topping out, then blessing and dedication, with Hewlett Thompson.

business. We had a lovely evening in the conservatory with Michael Mayne and Christopher Airy swapping behind the scenes reminiscences of events at Westminster Abbey, etc.

The Courtyard was an even bigger project for us, and the set piece events were a good way to keep up morale on the long fund-raising slog. It was not uncommon to celebrate one stage in several different ways. The start of works ceremony in July 2001 involved the Lord Lieutenant of Devon, Eric Dancer, presenting builder Roy Peters with three tools for the job. A symbolic key to the site (now hanging in the Fat Pigeon), a framed artist's impression of the project (so he knew what to build) and a large teapot (to keep the workers supplied). Sarah was dismayed by the gender stereotyping when she was the one who got to hold the teapot for the press photo. During the July workweek we had a procession around the building and a mass cutting of the turf on what was

then a lawn and is now under the dining room. The youngest participant was Nicholas Summerfield at two years

old and the oldest, John Lawson in his nineties. When the Timber Frame Company finished the job of putting in the Great Barn's green oak frame we had an impromptu celebration. Apparently tradition dictates that a sprig of oak should be nailed to the top of the roof and this was duly accomplished, but we failed to arrange for the required 'local virgin' to carry out the task. Hillary baked a barn-shaped cake and we toasted with

champagne. The photo we took of the event was used in the next fund-raising flyer. It generated an anxious telephone call from the insurers enquiring what we were doing with someone on the roof without a hard hat, no fencing around the compound, and a woman with sticks on the building site. Red faces all round.

A Royal Visit

When the thatching was completed we were delighted to welcome the Duke of Gloucester for the official topping out ceremony. This was our first (and so far only) royal visit so we had to learn all the necessary protocols in setting it up. It was disconcerting to realise the police were

LEFT: Courtyard start of works ceremony, including Roy Peters, Eric Dancer, Michael Langrish and Mary Weatherley.

ABOVE and LEFT: Cutting the first turf ceremony for the Courtyard.

ABOVE: Jim Blackburn cutting the Great Barn topping out cake.

BELOW: Members of the Community meeting the Duke of Gloucester.

armed. We prepared a special bound presentation book to give to the duke, and souvenir copies to those who had especially helped us with setting up the visit. We were pleased to share the day with representatives from a number of trusts who were supporting the project. Publicity photos are an important part of any such event and Karen Taylor snapped us at every turn. The duke was of course used to such exposure and looked serenely interested at all times, but we had wicked fun with a caption competition with the out-takes of ourselves pulling all sorts of unseemly faces. The focus of the event was presenting the duke with a straw bird for thatcher Mike Dray to set up on the top of the roof. The birds are often seen in this area

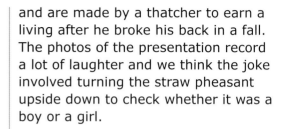

and are made by a thatcher to earn a living after he broke his back in a fall. The photos of the presentation record a lot of laughter and we think the joke involved turning the straw pheasant upside down to check whether it was a boy or a girl.

One of the fund-raising events for the Courtyard was Exeter Voices for St Cecilia in Exeter cathedral. Jonathan Williams spotted that Nigel Perrin was conducting the Exeter Festival Chorus. Nigel had led some young people's workshops at Sheldon when he left the King's Singers. Carl had always wanted to stage a musical event on the festival day of St Cecilia, patron saint of music, and reckoned that combining Exeter's two biggest and best choirs for the first time in Exeter cathedral was the way to do it. Andrew Millington and Nigel Perrin rose to the challenge with a magnificent programme. Our invited front row guests all wore evening dress to make the occasion more grand, and Carl and Sarah presented huge bouquets to Andrew and Nigel at the end of the concert. The cathedral was almost full, and we raised £6,000 for the appeal and generated lots of publicity.

After five long years of planning, fund-raising and construction, the completion of the Courtyard definitely merited a very big celebration. The official event took place on the wettest

possible day and we all got ecstatically soaked. Eric Dancer did the official opening, receiving the key to the site back from Roy Peters and presenting it to Carl. The plaque outside the Great Barn porch was unveiled. Bishop Michael Langrish did the dedication, and then all the assembled company set off round the building. The Panama Jazz Band gave a rousing rendition of 'He's got the whole world in his hands' (verse two: He's got the Courtyard in his hands) as we processed with incense swung, holy water sprinkled, and stopping for blessings by a different bishop at each door (Richard Hawkins, Peter Ball, Michael Ball). Bishop Richard's cope had a lovely red silk lining and in the rain the colour ran all over his alb.

In the long wet winter of 2001 when there was a lot of demolition, a lot of money being spent, and not much coming in, Sarah declared that she would 'refuse to turn forty until I can do it in the Courtyard'. The comment

ABOVE: *Exeter Voices for St Cecilia in the cathedral.*

caused much mirth and a party was duly promised. In August 2003 a joint party was held in the completed Courtyard to thank the builders for all their hard work, and to celebrate Sarah's fortieth birthday on schedule. With his penchant for fireworks, Carl arranged to have a six cannon salute fired for the builders, and the building/birthday cake was piped in by the City of Plymouth Pipe Band. It didn't take long to discover how good the new facilities were for parties (as well as all the other worthy uses for which we had purportedly built them).

Birthday Honours

We are very used to keeping confidences, but one of the hardest ones was that Carl had been awarded

LEFT: *Opening of the Courtyard including Roy Peters and Eric Dancer.*

ABOVE: Courtyard Blessing and Dedication

very expensive), Carl requested that his investiture take place at Sheldon where he could share it with the Community and friends. The very formal ceremony duly took place in the very rustic setting of the Animal Barn at the end of the Annual Eucharist. Three young trumpeters provided a fanfare for the occasion.

By comparison with the Courtyard, the building of the Pig Pens was a tiny project, but it still merited several events. The first was a select appeal launch in March 2005 aided and abetted by Petronella the piggy bank. Next, Christopher Airy gamely donned a hard hat and picked up a sledge hammer to take a symbolic first swipe at the old chalets during the November workparty weekend. We failed to tell him that the main front frame had been taken out and propped back in place so he got a bit of a shock when the whole thing fell in at the first hit.

the MBE in the Queen's birthday honours in 2002. We threw a party for the occasion but couldn't say on the invitation what it was for as it was only to be announced that day. We laid on a few surprises for Carl like a special haiku written by Richard Skinner, and all toasted Carl and the empire. With ticket numbers very restricted at Buckingham Palace (and the trip

Archbishop's visit

Carl noticed that Rowan Williams, Archbishop of Canterbury, would be consecrating the new bishop of Plymouth at Exeter cathedral in December 2005. We invited him for tea at Sheldon afterwards and to our delight he accepted, and agreed to bless the foundations of the Pig Pens. In preparing the words to be said by the archbishop, the staff at Lambeth

RIGHT: A toast to welcome Carl to Membership of the British Empire in 2002.

Palace only discovered late in the day that the Pig Pens were actually for human habitation. The event nearly ended in disaster when the archbishop was saying prayers and sprinkling holy water on the foundations, and only narrowly avoided a sprinkling from on high himself. The plumbers were sorting out the pipework to the upstairs toilet in the Long Barn, which was temporarily disconnected because the outflow pipe would come down through the Pig Pens roof. With the disconnected pipe twenty feet above ground a bucket of (thankfully clean) water was inadvertently tipped down the system, and only just missed the archepiscopal head. We all laughed from surprise, but were quite upset that something like that should happen to any guest at Sheldon, and it must have been really quite unnerving for him.

The opening of the Pig Pens was set up for Easter Monday 2006. Delays with delivery of the front frames meant that construction was behind schedule, and the builders wanted the opening put back a few weeks. With invitations already sent out and the event set up, we decided to go ahead anyway, ready or not. In the event, the builders left on Good Friday and the workparty volunteers spent the weekend frantically cleaning and kitting out the Berkshire Pig Pen as a 'show home'. The curtains were up and the bed was made and it really looked quite good. We also got the garden area rotavated, manured, weed-matted, gravelled and planted up over the weekend. We rather liked the processing around the building bit, so we did that again with help from a Newton Abbot band. Jonathan Meyrick, dean of Exeter, led

BELOW: Rowan Williams discussing the Mary and Martha ministry in a Linhay Lodge.

prayers and blessings, including an ingenious collect on a porcine theme. We invited three friends to open a Pig Pen each – Sir Christopher Airy, Rosemary Howell and Bishop Peter Ball. The store at the end is called the Piglet and Hillary solemnly opened that. As soon as the ceremony and lunch were over all the furnishings were whisked out again for the builders to complete the final week of work.

In July 2007 the extension to the Animal Barn was finished and we hadn't yet managed a party for Carl's 60th birthday, so we reckoned that

a Barn Extension opening party was called for. Street Heat samba band drummed us up to the barn where Eric Dancer opened the tractor shed and his wife Carole opened the sheep shed. Tractors were revved up and sheep were paraded in pink ribbons before the birthday boy was toasted and we all tucked into a good meal.

We couldn't list all the other parties and events, but here are just a few: A dinner in a marquee for seventy people for the tenth anniversary of the local village twinning (Bridford with St Vaast sur Seulles) in 1987. Wedding

RIGHT: Procession up the new path for the opening and blessing of the Pig Pens, including William Parker, Christopher Airy, Peter Ball and Rosemary Howell, Mary Weatherley and Jonathan Meyrick.

LEFT: Opening the Animal Barn with Eric and Carole Dancer.

receptions for Adrian and Ilse Canvin, and Kustan McRae and Pete. Plenty of birthdays - Sarah Lee's 18th, Carl's 40th, Jan's 40th (sixties dress code), Sue's 60th, Mary Weatherley's 70th and Gwen Lee's 80th. A 90th birthday party combined Bob Smith's 50th and Lindsey Bolton's 40th for an hysterical karaoke evening. Cakes baked, food prepared, furniture moved, bottles uncorked, speeches made, music played.

We enjoyed an appreciative comment from a friend 'Sheldon sure knows how to throw a good party'.

LEFT: Sue blowing out her birthday cake candles assisted by grandson Sam and sister Helen.

The Theatre

Building the theatre

When Carl was sent particulars of Sheldon with a view to working here, the black and white promotional leaflet included a map showing the 'theatre' in the grounds. With his track record of staging flamboyant events this certainly attracted him to come and take a look. So imagine his reaction on a frosty morning in March, dressed in his Church Army uniform and unsuitable shoes, peering over the bank to see the theatre for the first time. What does he see? An amphitheatre-shaped hillside covered in bracken and brambles with a boggy pond at the bottom. But as with so many things, he could 'see the potential' (as well as worrying about the Trades Descriptions Act). That week Carl sketched out some notes of things he would like to do if he came to Sheldon – the swimming pool never materialised, but the theatre has been close to Sheldon's heart ever since.

Colin Ward was Carl's first true ally in making the theatre a reality. With an architectural training behind him, he came up with the idea of building a wooden stage over the bog. Although the design was eventually deemed impractical because of the damp environment making a slippery surface, and the prospect of swarms of midges on summer nights, the flame had been lit.

RIGHT: Mike Gardner laying turfs in the theatre ~ 1980.

BELOW: Carl building the stone wall along the theatre top path with Andy Leigh.

The following year, in October 1977, Carl went down to the putative theatre with the newly arrived Mike Gardner. The environmental experiment damming the stream to form a bog had to go. They got filthy wet, muddy and sweaty as they opened the dam, and dug a channel through the silt to allow the bog to drain. Sadly there are no photos in the archive to record the historic day. Next, a set of 45 gallon oil drums sourced from Teignmouth docks were laid end to end in the channel to carry the stream through. The accounts department was surprised to get a bill for a lorry load of ready mixed concrete soon after the Church Army bought Sheldon, but by then there was no stopping the momentum of the project. Formal approval was the sort of detail that didn't trouble Carl too much, and in any case it wasn't long before glossy photos of performances were adorning reception at the Church Army's London HQ. The concrete to form the culvert taking the

stream under the stage was pushed down the steep bank in a corrugated iron chute with the help of lots of local young volunteers. One later load of readymix was dumped outside the chapel by an unhelpful driver making for some manic hard work to shift it before it set solid. Clinker from the forge at Dunsford iron mills was carted down to help build up the stage area. Now that the theatre was really taking shape, it was something that people wanted to get involved in. In those days everything was done manually – we wheeled barrows loaded with stone, gravel, cement etc up and down the steep paths. In the early years electric cables were simply laid on the surface, but soon we were digging a network of trenches burying everything underground.

ABOVE: Comfort ye my People in 1978.

LEFT: Mike Gardner and Andy Leigh building the steps down the side of the theatre early 1980s.

ABOVE: Posters for the four years of theatre company summer seasons.

RIGHT: Children of the Free.

Peter Harflett had recently moved to Doddiscombsleigh to help renovate Lake House. Bringing his architectural skills on to the scene he pegged out how we might dig out the terraces for people to sit on. These were all dug and turfed by hand (occasionally in the wrong direction hence the quirky angles in some places) and have been lovingly cared for ever since. The building of the theatre was a long term project, occupying us for many Easter and summer workparties over the best part of twenty years. A dressing room was needed, but the ground was too wet, so without any suitable engineering qualifications we built a concrete raft that is still doing good service 25 years later. The original dressing room was built mainly with wood offcuts from a firm making garden sheds near Bow, and was replaced with a more solid edition several decades later. Assessing the tall retaining wall of the stage the local officer from the Royal Engineers declared 'that will never work' – but the handiwork of Carl, Sarah, Phil Hutchins and Karen Peters hasn't cracked yet. Chris Cockman built the burger bar, box office and various walls. Jim Pilkington built the control box, judged by the surveyor to be Victorian in style (too solid ever to be demolished). Ernie Townsend was the only professional bricklayer and he taught many volunteers essential skills. Barry Amis and Tez

LEFT: The Godspell band rehearsing in the old workshop at the back of the Great Barn.

Hastings were involved at various stages of installing sound and lighting equipment. In the early days we had a lot of help from David and Graham who were setting up Stage Electrics operating out of cramped premises underneath the iron bridge in Exeter. It is now one of the biggest sound and light companies in the country.

BELOW: A colourful performance of Godspell, including Paul Welch, Nuala Forsythe, Gail Bruce and Jenny Haines.

Early performances

BELOW: Robert Runcie's
commendation at the
official opening of the
theatre.

The first ever performance was The
Insect Play, performed by the Teign
Valley Junior Players on 21st and 22nd
July 1978 - all seats priced at 50p.
Theatre audiences have always imbued
the occasions with a great deal of
goodwill, which is part of the magic of
the place. In the early days, audience
members often included friends and
family of the performers, and people
who had helped with the work of
creating the theatre itself. The growing
housechurch movement in Exeter
was a source of faithful and generous
support for a number of years. The
Sheldon Theatre Company came
together in 1978 led by Carl and Guy
Pierce. Mike Gardner was the theatre's
technical Mr Fixit. Each production was
conceived and written by the company,
with meetings throughout the winter
months to develop ideas, followed

The Archbishop of Canterbury

"There has been one Archbishop of Canterbury who might have been
described as a theatrical entrepreneur. His name, curiously, was Gilbert
Sheldon, so I feel a small historical echo in my delight at the opening of your
theatre. It is an impressive achievement, and all the more remarkable for being
the work of volunteers. I hope that many of those who have worked so hard and
for so long will return to enjoy what they have created.
Many congratulations, and my prayers and best wishes for your success in the
future"

Robert Cantuar

by residential writing and rehearsing weekends at Sheldon during the spring and early summer. Four or five performances were staged at weekly intervals in July and August, often with audiences of 500 or so. At a time when the Greenbelt festival was in its infancy, and the Christian drama and music scene was very limited, it was an immensely exciting and innovative project. Much hard work was invested, and it was a time of great spiritual growth for many of those involved. Bridget Boxall led the dance input, Andy Hague and Lou Lewis the music,

LEFT: A typically stoic audience enjoying Acker Bilk and his Paramount Jazz Band from under their umbrellas in 1987.

and Tim Haines the technical side. Comfort ye my People was the first in 1978, followed by Children of the Free the next year. After Guy left Max Carpenter took over as director and

LEFT: The Spinners on their Final Fling tour in 1988. Bands had much less PA kit to be carried up and down the theatre in those days.

ABOVE: Springs Dance Company in 1990.

The Vineyard and then Messengers followed in 1980 and 1981. Many lasting friendships were forged and an amazing amount of talent was showcased within this unique company. For those responsible for the practical hard graft of creating the theatre, the moments when the audience settled, the music started, the lights came on, and a performance was under way never failed to send a tingle down the spine. That magical buzz of people coming together has continued as the theatre has evolved.

The middle years

RIGHT: Steve Thompson leading a workweekend team rolling up the theatre carpet in 1992.

In 1984 we eventually got round to having an official opening of the theatre. Christian rockstar Randy Stonehill was flown in from America

to perform, and a celebratory open afternoon included entertainment from Larry Grayson, Jimmy Cricket, the Exeter University Singers and the Exeter British Rail Brass Band. The souvenir brochure included supportive comments from church and theatre luminaries of the day like Roy Castle and the Archbishop of Canterbury.

Once the theatre company had disbanded we began staging more music concerts interspersed with drama as opportunities arose. With an outdoor setting the weather is always an unpredictable variable. Acker Bilk and his Paramount Jazz Band twice performed in a downpour in the middle of otherwise bone dry summers. Carl remembers going on stage to face a sea of audience umbrellas to call off one of their performances that was losing the battle with the elements. True to the good nature of Sheldon audiences, they clapped, cheered and jigged their brollies when he told them to go home. In some years we put up a marquee on the Pound House lawn

as an alternative venue. Bands and singer-songwriters of all varieties have entertained audiences, and brought thousands of people into contact with Sheldon. Martyn Joseph deserves a special mention for his marathon run of concerts.

The natural setting of the theatre made for some obvious production choices. One of these was The Woodland Gospels staged by Flashpoint theatre company in 1985. People frequently suggest A Midsummer Night's Dream and this was indeed performed by the Teign Valley Players in 1997. One of the most popular productions was a lively and colourful version of Godspell directed by David Ash in 1986.

Looking back at these middle years, although there wasn't always quite the energy and flair of the early days, the theatre was still serving as an important link between Sheldon and the wider community. It is easy for a bunch of Christians living at the end of a no-through road to be regarded with suspicion and even hostility by those in the locality. Having learned tough lessons in the isolation of his very early days Carl has always been keen to ensure that Sheldon nurtures healthy connections with the local community. It is fascinating how often visitors (like a burly man recently delivering scaffolding for a building

ABOVE: Alvin Stardust performing in the marquee in 1987.

project) will light up with enthusiasm at their memories of attending or being involved with building the theatre a couple of decades ago. It is wonderful to think how many lives the theatre has touched.

Other theatre snippets from the communal memory-bank:
• Children from Woodbury Salterton school in residence for a week rehearsing and then performing to parents a play on the 2000 eclipse, including a Chinese dragon and drumming that reverberated for days.
• An atmospherically misty night during the Seedpack youth weekend in 1982 with Steve Chalk and Keith Loring among those performing as Anagram.

• Carl getting a big cheer as he fired five red 'gerbs' at the front of the stage to create a wall of smoke for a scene change in The Vineyard.
• Rock and Roll legend Alvin Stardust being joined on stage by a nonplussed Ginger the cat.
• The Spinners arguing backstage before singing of love and harmony on one of their many farewell tours.
• An Evening under the Son with Adrian Snell and mime artist Geoffrey Stevenson, both battling food poisoning from a dodgy meal at a local pub the night before.
• David Kossoff telling bible stories to 600 spellbound children.
• The Royal Marines' Bandmaster being surprised to get answers to his rhetorical questions from learning disabled youngsters in the audience – all taken smoothly in hand by fellow audience member Larry Grayson.

Other artists have included Pam Ayres, The Cambridge Buskers, Randy Stonehill, The Fairer Sax and Mark II.

Renaissance

The theatre went through a fallow period once we were heavily immersed

RIGHT: The theatre re-opens in 2004 with the Fab Beatles.

in building projects like the Courtyard. We simply didn't have the time and energy required to run the theatre as well. It was also the era of increasing health and safety regulation of public entertainments, and much of the early electrical equipment was coming to the end of its useful life. The choice had to be made whether to let the theatre revert to nature, or to invest judiciously in the future of this hidden gem. Some people felt it didn't particularly fit with Sheldon's core ministry, while others felt that a unique community resource should not be allowed to fall into disrepair. Carl continued to believe in the value of the theatre as a gentle form of outreach and began to gather a volunteer theatre team to manage the staffing of concert nights. From 2003 we began re-investing in the theatre with a new dressing room, upgrading of the electrical installation and house lights to meet modern standards, conversion to digital sound and light systems, upgrading of the burger bar, an improved car parking area, and an easy access platform for disabled guests. And of course we did the risk assessments, wrote the staff training manual, rehearsed our emergency procedures, and obtained a premises licence. In 2004 we were delighted to see the theatre back in action with a full-throttle trip down memory lane from local tribute band The Fab Beatles. The

2005 season included more band gigs, Gordon Haskell and an incredibly moving passion play staged by the Melanesian Brotherhood as part of their six week mission in the diocese of Exeter. Earlier in the day children from Doddiscombsleigh primary school had walked across the fields from the village for a special music workshop with the brothers. It was a delight to see the barriers of race and culture melt away as the brothers taught them the Devon duck dance and the afternoon ended with a touchingly emotional rendition of Thankyou for the Music from the children. 2006 was the driest theatre season on record as the valley pulsated to the Fab Beatles, dIRE tRAITS, '80s glam rock from Diamondogz, and Sinatra era music

ABOVE: Theatre team in uniform in 2006 including Tez Hastings, Phil Hutchins, David Peters, Jim Pilkington, Tony and Pauline Mortimer, John Hall and Adrian Canvin.

from a sharp-suited nine piece Rat Pack. 2007 was the wettest summer on record, but we still managed to stage all four concerts as planned. The extra mud added some Glastonbury-style panache to the proceedings, and the Beach Boys Inc eventually managed to cheer up and bring their trademark soundtrack of summer to a damp Devon night.

Perhaps the last word should go to Carl and Sue's grandaughter Charlotte turning to her parents during a concert and exclaiming 'They're live aren't they?' What a great gift to offer real music in an atmospheric natural setting to the next generation growing up in a world of virtual entertainment.

RIGHT: A stark and emotionally powerful crucifixion scene from the Melanesian Mission's The Passion of our Lord in 2005. An ambulance was called to an elderly member of the audience who lost consciousness. On coming round she apologised to the paramedics 'I suppose you don't see a crucifixion every day'.

LEFT: The Royal Marines' Big Band beaing the retreat in the camping field after a concert in the theatre in July 2000.

The Capek brothers' 'The Insect Play' which Jean Hughes directed was the first production by the Teign Valley Junior Players, at Sheldon, on July 21/22nd 1978; all seats were priced at 50p! On June 6/7th 1986 (admission £1) was my own adaptation and direction of Kenneth Graham's book 'The Wind in the Willows'. The increased admission charge enabled us to cover production costs and make a donation of £65 to Sheldon funds. Of particular value over 19 years were the regular summer workshops at Sheldon. These were held over one or two days with rehearsals, a picnic lunch and tea, opportunity to run off surplus energy and then a performance to parents in the early evenings. It was the greatest pleasure for all of us, in fine weather, to enjoy the fresh air and sunshine, happy activity and the beauty of the amphitheatre setting: Junior Players were very lucky to have this facility available. In August 1987, after a 2 day workshop, members performed a dramatization of Robert Browning's famous poem 'The Pied Piper of Hamlin' and in August 1988 a programme of 3 plays 'The Stolen Prince', 'The Cutting of Marchan Wood' (with music) and 'Sunday Costs Five Pesos'. In 1993 on July 3rd, we held a Summer Saturday at Sheldon, with games and rehearsal for a late afternoon performance of a Russian fable 'The Nosebag', for all 21 members of what had become Junior Drama in the Teign Valley. Fundraising performances for local causes were a part of Junior Drama activity. In 1989 the entire membership joined in giving two performances of a programme of four short plays: 'Absolutely Nothing', 'The Pardonner's Tale', 'Harlequinade' (mime) and, with parents playing some of the parts, 'These Boots are made for Walking'. These performances were Junior Drama's own contribution to fund raising for the Teign Valley Community Hall. In 1990, on Saturday July 21st, older members performed 'Calypso Market' in a programme devised by local people to raise funds for the Acorn Community Support Group. Members of Junior Drama in the Teign Valley took part in two of the three adult productions which raised funds for the Teign Valley Community Hall. In the 1995 production of 'The Roses of Eyam', by Don Taylor, there was an introduction, based on children's singing games, specially devised for them, before the play proper began. In 1997 they took part as the Fairies in William Shakespeare's 'A Midsummer Night's Dream'. These plays, together with Shakespeare's 'Twelfth Night' in 1999, were all independent productions put on with invaluable help from Hillary at Sheldon, who collected together the information, laid out and printed the programmes, organized the printing of tickets and their sale on the door and publicised the performances. With happy memories of the splendid Sheldon years and very best wishes. Marilyn Chapman.

Working the land

Sourcing accurate information about who has owned and lived at Sheldon is quite a challenge. The property deeds were destroyed by a direct hit on the records office in Exeter during the second world war. Perhaps one day someone with time on their hands and internet access will be able to do some serious research and enlighten us all.

Early records

The earliest records show Sheldon belonging to a family, possibly called Bayley or Bailey. A Robert Bayly who died in 1653 is noted as having had 'his lands in Doddiscombsleigh sequestered for recusancy on 19 February 1646'. As a Roman Catholic he was committing the

RIGHT: Aerial photo in 1966.

ABOVE: Aerial photo in 2004.

statutory offence of not complying with the established Church of England. According to Prebendary Buckingham's history of the parish of Doddiscombsleigh, the catholic family at Sheldon had died out by 1742.

The tax records for 1780 to 1831 refer to Shildon and begin to give us more information about the inhabitants of the farm. It appears that for much of the last two hundred or more years it has been owned by absentee landlords and farmed by tenants. Many were called Archer or Sercombe, both common local names. Samuel and Elizabeth Archer farmed at Sheldon in 1841, with

ABOVE: Olive Sercombe (left) celebrating her 90th birthday with her family in the Community Kitchen in 1996.

their daughter Mary and son William, who inherited the tenancy. In 1851 he is noted as a single man, head of the household, and farming 130 acres with the aid of a housekeeper and four resident servants. By 1861 William had reduced the holding to 120 acres and recorded three men and two boys as employees. William was unmarried but another Samuel Archer and his wife Mary Jane, aged 26 and 30, are noted as the young tenants in 1871. They had added a further thirty acres and employed three men and a boy. What happened to bring George and Emma Dolbeare, also young tenants, into the records in 1881? In 1891, the Sercombes of Bridford appear at Sheldon. Joseph and Mary Ann had eight children, several

listed as 'scholar' in the census data. However, this Sercombe family were only distantly related to the Sercombe family of the 1960s.

From 1891, information again becomes more scanty, as personal data is not released for a hundred years. We know that a family called Passmore lived here after the first world war, at which time the South Wing was derelict and tumble-down. Some say it fell down, others that it was destroyed by fire. The tithe map and apportionments of 1838 lists the fields belonging to Sheldon by name. What is now the car park was known as the Stable Orchard; the camping field was Little Field Top of Copse; the area behind the house was the Little Orchard and Home Orchard; our large field beyond the animal barn was Down Park and Gulf and Yonder Orchard; in front of the Pig Pens and Long Barn was known as Teign Orchard.

Living memory

From talking to Olive Sercombe when she was a redoubtable lady in her nineties, we know that she and her husband Billy first rented Sheldon from Mr Surridge of Bridford Mills in 1946. He died in 1958 and the following year they were able to buy the farm of a hundred acres. Olive and Billy brought up a family here. Their son Alan remembers shearing

LEFT: Carl mowing the Prayer Meadow in the barn field in 2004.

Percheron mare because there were still some jobs that a horse did better than a tractor. The farm buildings were surrounded by apple orchards and every autumn the apples were bagged up and sent off to Whiteways for pressing for cider. Billy kept a vegetable garden where the carpark is now. Olive bought day old chicks to rear as capons in the shippen and kept free range geese and ducks which she took to Newton Abbot on the train from Christow station (at the end of the Sheldon lane) on market day. In 1966 Olive and Billy decided to retire owing to his poor health and Alan's offer of a job with the Heltor oil company. Sadly Billy was not able to

BELOW: Taking hay off the barn field after the Prayer Meadow ended.

sheep in the Great Barn - they kept a hundred Greyface Dartmoors, the same breed we brought back to Sheldon in 2005. Pigs were bought in batches of twenty weaners and fattened over eight months in the Pigsties. They kept about 35 cattle of the local South Devon breed. Most were store cattle for beef, but two were milked by hand in what is now the quiet room end of the Pound House (then the shippen) to provide milk and cream for the household. All the cattle were overwintered in the Linhay. The two shire horses Prince and Colonel were stabled in the Great Barn but their days were numbered with the purchase of a tractor in 1947. The next year Billy traded them in for a dappled

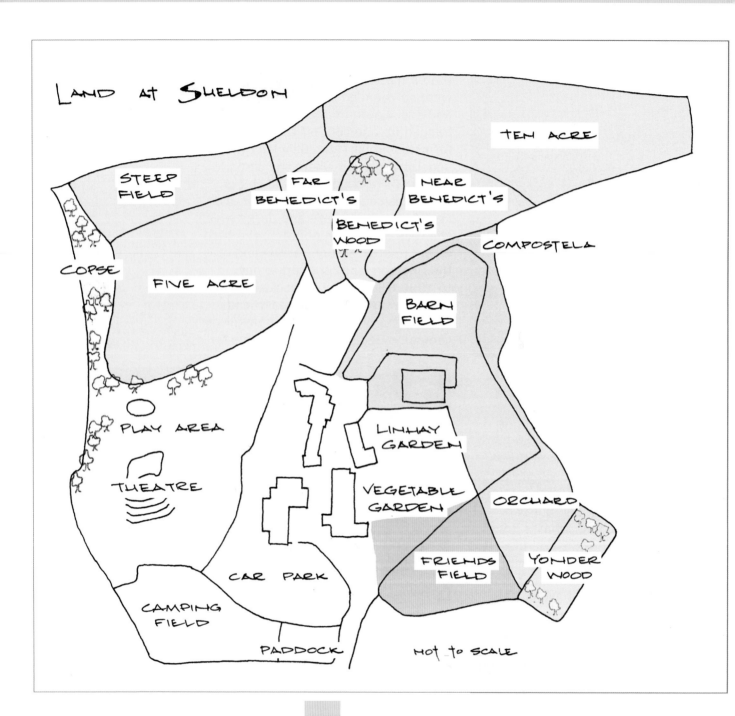

Land at Sheldon

TEN ACRE

STEEP FIELD

FAR BENEDICT'S

NEAR BENEDICT'S

BENEDICT'S WOOD

COMPOSTELA

COPSE

FIVE ACRE

BARN FIELD

PLAY AREA

LINHAY GARDEN

THEATRE

VEGETABLE GARDEN

ORCHARD

CAR PARK

FRIENDS FIELD

YONDER WOOD

CAMPING FIELD

PADDOCK

NOT TO SCALE

enjoy retirement as he died later the same year. Olive retained occasional contact with Sheldon until her death in 2007 aged 101.

Dividing the farm

The Sercombes sold Sheldon to Geoffrey and Mary Fraser for £5,400 in 1966 when Geoffrey was vicar of Dunsford. In a same-day transaction most of the land was sold off, retaining the buildings and about 38 acres. Geoffrey sold Sheldon to the Church Army for £37,000 in 1977 but retained Coombes Cottage and the railway leaving Sheldon with just twelve acres. The purchase was supported with a loan from the Girls' Friendly Society who held the deeds until SMM bought Sheldon for £210,000 in 1991. Several neighbouring parcels of land, all of which formed part of the earlier holding, have since been bought back.

Buying back

The first purchase was the Barn Field in 1992. It had been owned by Jim and Eileen Harvey at Lowley who were good friends and agricultural advisers in Carl and Sue's early days. Eileen had grown up at Sheldon being the daughter of Billy and Olive Sercombe. Lowley was bought by Bill King and then by Arnold and Christine Underhay as part of their 'thousand acres in the Teign valley' expansion. We bought

the Barn Field, plus Yonder Wood from them for £24,000. This was the first step in dividing the Sheldon grounds into areas open to everyone (including noisy children), and areas set aside for people needing quiet retreat. It gave us five acres of additional grazing together with a small section of oak woodland thought to have been planted in the mid 1800s as commercial timber. The buildings had been hard up against the east boundary of the site, and now started to have a bit more breathing space.

Next door to Sheldon is Coombes Cottage. Back in the 1970s it was little more than a wooden shed owned by

BELOW: Carl leading the way for the blessing of the Spanishlake land after the Annual Eucharist in 2005, including Mike and Oliver Gardner and Roy Walford.

a Mr Coombe who used to work on
the railway. With a certain amount
of refurbishment it was used as a
venue for the youth club which Carl
ran during his first year at Sheldon.
Geoffrey Fraser sold Coombes Cottage
to Keith and Mary Wakley along
with two small fields and part of the
old railway line. Keith was a skilled
stonemason who rebuilt the hut as
their family home. He and Mary kept
poultry and pigs and were good friends
and neighbours to us.

In 1988 the Wakleys moved on to
convert the old sawmills at nearby
Kennick, and John and Elsie Neville
bought Coombes Cottage. They made
extensive additions to the house,
built a range of aviaries for their

parrots, lined the lane with Lawson's
Cypress and generally urbanised
their environment. One of the worst
features of their tenure was the speed
bumps which suddenly appeared on
the lane outside their house. There
were also various boundary disputes,
and we were especially worried when
the boundary fence to our back garden
was unilaterally re-positioned to within
yards of the house. With plans under
way to build the Linhay we were
increasingly concerned about antisocial
behaviour and loss of privacy both for
ourselves and for guests.

Thanks to a legacy and the support of Friends of Mary and Martha we raised the exorbitant sum of £21,250 to buy the adjacent field from the Nevilles in 1997, and called it Friends' Field. Small, steep and south facing with a seasonal stream at the bottom of the slope, it provides a spring nursery area for ewes and young lambs and a regular route out of Sheldon for foraging badgers. It also enabled us to install a sewage treatment plant to serve the Linhay, and to move the vegetable garden down the hill to make room for the new Linhay garden. For the first time in two decades Sheldon had buildings completely surrounded by its own land.

The most recent, and biggest acquisition yet, was in November 2004. Sue spotted an advert in the local paper and we realised that the Underhays were starting the long-awaited sell-off of their extensive land holdings in the valley. For three years Carl had had a map pinned on the board in his office with a line drawn round what is now Five Acre, Steep Field and Benedict's Near, Far and Wood. With only a few weeks before sealed tenders were due in we called an emergency trustees' meeting and hammered out three bid options, of which the largest acreage proved successful. As with all our land purchases we did a lot of soul searching about spending £85,000

on land, but there was a sense of the rightness in making good use of land for people. We had to do a lot of creative application of available funds, loans and donations to make it possible. The fields are together referred to as Spanishlake after the farm that used to own them. The land had been badly neglected so there was plenty of work needed to tidy up sunken muddy gateways, install water troughs, maintain the hedges and manage the rampant thistles. The fields were fenced to provide walking paths for guests separate from the livestock. As part of the Underhay sell-off we did also look very seriously at another ten acre field with the pine tree clump which we look across to on the south side. At the time

BELOW: Taking delivery of three tonnes of manure for the garden – Sarah's birthday present from her Dad in 1986, including Sarah and Simon Lee, Paul Welch and Tez Hastings.

ABOVE: Planting the hedge along Orchard Way hedge during the winter workparty in 1997, including Nigel Bibbings and David Silk.

RIGHT: Simon Lee test driving the first ride on mower behind the Woodshed.

£45,000 was beyond our means and we also worried it might be viewed as accumulation for its own sake. Two years later it was bought by a land banking company now cynically selling 100 'building plots' at 7,000 euros each (do the math). We trust that a housing estate is not a credible threat, but we do wish we'd had the courage of our convictions and found that extra money somehow.

Caring for the land

Instead of serious farming our land is now managed as part of the overall ethos of Sheldon as a healing and holistic place, giving guests open spaces to walk, relax, unwind and let the natural world inspire and calm. There have been huge changes in the ways the work has been done. In the early years, Carl worked with students and volunteers, many of whom found themselves acquiring unexpected skills in the many tasks required to manage and maintain a rural site. Much of Sheldon was very overgrown - the garden behind the Farmhouse consisted almost entirely of brambles. Sheer hard labour gradually pushed back the boundaries of the jungle. Carl's original electric lawnmower only reached the length of its cable and soon succumbed to overwork. When Steve Thompson was here in the 1980s one of his tasks was cutting the grass outside the Pound House. One wet summer it got too rough and too long for any kind of mower so had to be cut with a strimmer and raked up by hand. After a series of petrol mowers, the first ride on lawn tractor was purchased in April 1995 thanks to a £1,500 grant from the Abel Trust. This made a huge difference to the amount of time it took to keep grass in order, and extended the area which

could be brought in hand and made easily accessible for guests. In more recent years we have been able to upgrade to bigger machines including compact tractors and attachments which also collect the grass. This has meant we can mow walkways around the further fields so that people can walk comfortably and still be amidst grasses and wild flowers. Catherine Heron spent one July workweek making a series of drawings to assemble into a pocket sized booklet to guide and prompt guests on a meditation walk around Sheldon.

LEFT: Terracing for the new vegetable garden in Friends' Field in 1997.

In 2000 we joined the Dartmoor Environmentally Sensitive Area scheme with a management plan for the grassland plus access to grants for maintenance of hedges and fences.

LEFT: The old vegetable garden in transition from builder's yard to Linhay garden during the summer of 1998.

Grassland has to be managed through grazing by sheep and cutting for hay in order to keep it in good order and enable a wide range of species to thrive. Minimal fertilizers have been used since 2001, and we are careful not to have so much stock that in winter the ground could be churned up and soil strata damaged.

Back in 1988 it was possible to obtain grants from the Manpower Services Commission for community enterprise projects. An MSC job creation scheme based at Sheldon trained clients in countryside and woodland skills. Coppicing is a traditional craft of cutting hazel on a five or seven year

rotation. Stands of hazel are cut to ground level, the cuttings used for hurdles, bean or walking sticks etc, and new growth soon begins to come up from the base of the stool. The project members built a bodger's hut complete with a wooden pole lathe, illustrating how furniture makers would have utilised the crop of wood. They also built three replica celtic huts in the copse. These were circular with wattle and daub walls and thatched roofs. Unfortunately the huts didn't last very long once children had discovered they could clamber up one side of the roof and slide gleefully down the other. The huts were eventually replaced by the current play area, a wooden platform with a rope climbing net, trap door and ramp, which was built by Chris Cockman.

BELOW: Carl with Simon and tomatoes in 1984.

We have a rolling programme of hedge maintenance where a different length is laid each winter. John Joslin, who retired from farming at nearby Bridford, laid several hundred yards of overgrown hedge in the winters of 2004 and 2006. Doing it gradually means that there are always sections of fully grown hedge available for nesting birds. Hedges are stock fenced to protect the banks from being eroded by exploring sheep. Since 1991 over five hundred metres of new hedges have been planted and established using traditional native Devon species of predominantly blackthorn and hawthorn with hazel, oak, spindle and holly. Hedges provide corridors for birds, mammals and insects to forage and move about in safety. They also provide us with a wild harvest of sloes (to make sloe gin) and elderflowers and berries for cordials and jellies. The woodland at Sheldon is managed on a minimal intervention basis to maintain the paths and keep a variety of habitats including open glades and areas of thick cover for wildlife.

ABOVE: Phil Searle and Chris Cockman landscaping behind the Farmhouse in 1989.

Wild flowers at Sheldon give much pleasure to visitors. Primroses are among the first of the spring flowers and early purple orchids are a special feature abundant in the old green lane and copse. The Teign valley is famous for wild daffodils and these too can be found in the copse. They are followed by wild garlic and bluebells, pink campion and yellow archangel. Meadow flowers such as sneezewort, ragged robin, meadowsweet, knapweed and trefoils are encouraged to flourish by cutting the grass later than usual so the wild flowers have time to seed.

Vegetable gardens

There have been two vegetable gardens at Sheldon in the lifetime

LEFT: Dedication of the mediterranean garden during workweek 1998.

ABOVE: Carl and Simon cutting through the old boundary from the barn field into the Spanishlake land in 2004.

RIGHT: Carl and Simon sowing the Pound House lawn in April 2003.

for 25 years although it did require the operator to understand its little peculiarities. Just as the rather poor soil was finally responding to tonnes of muck and constant working, so it had to be sacrificed to plans for the Linhay. It provided good material for the development of the Linhay gardens, with rose bed, rockery, borders and lawn. Some of the horseradish (it has big leaves like docks) from the old vegetable patch persisted in coming up through the new Linhay lawn for many years. Carl retained a corner of the original garden for his greenhouse and germination plot, and supervised the building of new and bigger walled

of this story. The first was where the Linhay garden is now, and was created from scratch with Carl in the role of chief gardener, later assisted by Sarah and a variety of volunteers. Raised beds were built, water pipes laid, and concrete mixed and poured for paths. It is a tradition at Sheldon that wet concrete should be decorated with footprints. Most of these belong to animals, including hens and ducks in their free range days, assorted cat and dog prints and the occasional human.

In 1980 Carl led a mission in Clevedon, and the parish wanted to make a practical gift. They presented us with a seriously sturdy rotavator which served

beds in the current vegetable garden created with the acquisition of Friends' Field. When Sarah's admin workload increased, Hillary stepped into her gardening wellies. Gradually the rough clay, shale and builders' rubble have been worked at with contributions from the donkeys, llamas and various local cattle and horses. Having started with one small shed and a tomato emporium greenhouse, we now have three greenhouses, a potting shed and a machine shed which is home to three freezers, small mowers, stocks of paint and assorted non-gardening tools. There is a permanent soft fruit area - rhubarb, blackcurrants, redcurrants, gooseberries and autumn raspberries do well here. We try to grow vegetables which we can produce in sufficient bulk to process and freeze for use when we cater for guests on events, and all kinds of beans come into this category. Carl grows barrowfuls of tomatoes (usually moneymaker and gardeners' delight) and Hillary grows a few more unusual varieties. Salad crops, courgettes, pumpkins, beetroot and leeks are other staples. We have difficulty growing strawberries and carrots, the favourite foods of the local badgers who have faultless timing in knowing precisely when they are at their best and mounting a night time raid on the vegetable garden.

ABOVE: Building the new entrance to the Courtyard in July 2002, including David Peters and Brian Marlow.

Landscaping

Every time there is a building project, there is landscaping and planting to go with it. Usually this entails turning the unpromising raw materials of a builders' yard into something presentable in double-quick time. We have learned plenty of handy tricks in the use of railway sleepers, weedmat, bark and gravel chippings, and lots and lots of manure. The shrubbery in front of the Linhay was so well manured it's now all we can do to keep it under control. By trying to reclaim the outside of a building as soon as the builders move inside we have generally been able to have things growing respectably before the official opening. Creating lawns has been a particular challenge. We rotavated

and stone-picked for three solid days before sowing the Linhay lawn, and the new Pig Pens lawn battled forlornly against the predations of rabbits in an exceptionally dry summer. The soil for the Pound House lawn came from the bottom of a local pond and was full of dock seed. As with the buildings, it can be hard to love the lawns into existence and then release them to be enjoyed, used and occasionally carelessly abused.

Hidden depths

Some features are connected with memories of loved relations or people for whom Sheldon was special. Others mark special occasions such as anniversaries or are connections with the recent past recycled into a new usefulness. The rambling rector rose is surely appropriate for the gardens of a house caring for people in ministry. Passion flowers with their beautiful symbolic blooms flourish around the edges of the Linhay garden, all descendants of one packet of seed sown to grow plants for sale in the early 1980s.

The present orchard at Sheldon was planted in 1998 in memory of Hillary's grandmother, with one tree in memory of Nigel Bibbings' father. The trees are traditional Devon varieties of apples, pears, plums and cherries on M25 rootstock which is slow to develop and will eventually make big old fashioned orchard trees. We have recently been enjoying the first fruiting years, although the birds have yet to allow us any cherries. The flowering cherry in the Linhay garden marked Carl and Sue's twenty five years at Sheldon. Lord and Lady Morley gave us a magnolia called heaven scent to mark the opening of the Linhay in 1999. The Pound House lawn is bordered by a hedge of white summer-flowering hebe loved by the bees, sheltering many rabbits and planted in memory of Sue's parents. The barn field has a row and a group of oak trees planted by Steve Thompson in 1993 to commemorate the fortieth anniversary of the Queen's accession to the throne.

There is a set of handsome granite stones forming the rockery in the Linhay garden. These came from the South Wing – the big slab was the front doorstep for nearly a hundred years, and the rest came from the chimney on the gable wall.

In the germination plot in the Linhay garden is a cross of pebbles set in concrete which was once part of the wall of the donkey pen in the old Linhay. In the top tread of the steps in the open air theatre another pebble cross was laid on Good Friday by the workparty which built that flight of steps.

There are a few artifacts from Sheldon's farming past. Outside the Farmhouse is a bench made out of a rough piece of granite which was one of the old farm gateposts and is known as Great Peter. Outside the Pig Pens are the remains of a hay grab and old farm ploughs and tines. See the outline of the one-horse single share plough to understand why the constellation ursa major is sometimes called the plough.

There are several benches around the Sheldon site which were given in memory of loved ones. Sarah and Jan chose to place the bench with stunning views at the top of ten acre field in memory of their sisters Alice and Sylvia. The bench at Compostela at the top of the barn field, commemorates Steve Thompson with his catch phrase 'All good fun' – usually when things

LEFT: Carl and Hillary marking out for fences and gates on Spanishlake Dec 2004.

BELOW: View of Sheldon from Woodah field in the 1960s.

RIGHT: Digging the new water main through Blackdown clump in August 1999. This is the field that has recently been land banked.

were anything but fun. Others were given by family and friends in memory of Lesley Buck and Muriel Ash, who loved to visit Sheldon. Those who take the path into Yonder Wood cross the stream by a simple wooden footbridge in memory of Margaret Pike.

Those who explore some of the hidden corners of Sheldon find statues and figures in unexpected places. The small stone figure carved by Geoffrey Fraser may represent an angel, or a supplicating figure with hands up-raised – Oliver Twist? a communicant at the altar rail? For many years it featured on the front cover of the Sheldon brochure in its position outside the Pound House and it is now on the corner of the Great Barn. In Yonder Wood a small statue of St Antony holding a child can be glimpsed amidst

BELOW: Simon Lee and Rom Dobbs landscaping in front of the Pig Pens in 2006.

the trees. St Francis welcomes those who find their way to the swing seat in dingly dell and a little further up the hill is St Cecilia's seat and wind chimes. The eye of the beholder made by sculptor Angela Holmes from Chudleigh greets those who explore the gravel garden outside the Pig Pens. A grinding stone is sunk into the wall of the theatre box office.

Water

The pump handle which once used to pump water from the well behind the Farmhouse is still in the Linhay

garden. In the days before the arrival of mains water, the farm depended on this well and on two more in Near Benedict's field up the hill beyond Sheldon. None of these were reliable in very dry weather and during the Sercombe's time here Sheldon was connected to a mains water supply. Even this was somewhat erratic as the three quarter inch pipe crossed several fields and two streams before reaching the garden behind the house. When pressure was low no water reached up to the top of the Long Barn and there were frequent neighbourly difficulties over paying for the shared supply, and especially for leaks along its length.

In 1999 we paid for the installation of a three inch main following the same route from the Doddiscombsleigh road, but this time with a meter (and just as importantly a fire hydrant) right in our back garden.

ABOVE: Drawing of Geoffrey Fraser's statue on the front cover of the 1960s Sheldon brochure pack.

LEFT: Aerial view of Sheldon in the 1980s.

Animal magic

No story of Sheldon would be complete without a mention of its furred and feathered inhabitants.

Poultry

On their first day at Sheldon the resident geese refused to let Carl and Sue venture out of the Pound House. Geese have not been kept at Sheldon since. However, an assortment of chickens and ducks have lent a farmyard atmosphere to the place over the years. Muscovy ducks came and went, finding life on the nearby river more attractive, but we have also kept Aylesbury, Call, Khaki campbell and Indian runner ducks. Thanks to the attentions of Mr Fox there were many years when we could not let the poultry run free-range. Their special fort knox run near the carpark did also make it rather easier to find the egg supplies. The latest arrivals are a trio

ABOVE: Steve Thompson with a favourite duckling.

RIGHT: Free-range hens and ducks in 1992 with Nichola and Jo Watson.

of unusual Blue laced cochin chickens (cockerel known as Elvis), which have fluffy feathers and feathery legs and feet. In 2007 the hens were relocated to moveable arks in the field where they have expressed their appreciation of the conditions by laying extra eggs. They have even been able to enjoy a short free-range outing each day and so far the fox hasn't noticed.

Sheep and goats

Also among the earlier inhabitants were the goats, occupying the Linhay before the humans. Ethel, Hereward and Tulip were followed by Flora, Mary and Twinkle. The goats were succeeded by an assortment of sheep, (among them a pair known as Sackcloth and Ashes) usually bought in spring as orphan lambs from local farms, reared through the summer and dispatched in the autumn. One year we had three lambs from Alice Horsman's farm in Dorset – Rachel, Ruth and Rebecca. As they were all

LEFT: Children feeding Rachel, Ruth and Rebecca outside the old Linhay.

ewes, we decided to keep and breed from them. Rachel resolutely refused to accept the attentions of a variety of handsome rams over the years, remaining a single lady of enormous size and earning her keep as aunt and companion to single rams or groups of junior sheep. Ruth and Rebecca produced a variety of offspring, including Pearl who contributed charming twins, one black and one white, to the photograph albums. With the acquisition of the barn field we decided to expand the flock to take advantage of and manage the extra grass. Hillary had an interest in rare breeds so she choose to keep Manx Loaghtans, a small brown primitive breed from the Isle of Man which can have two or four horns. The flock has

LEFT: Hillary with Pearl and the twins in the barn field in April 2000.

ABOVE: Hannah arriving at Sheldon, with Hillary, Sue, Clare Ward and Paul Welch.

LEFT: Flora, Mary and Twinkle in the old Linhay in the 1980s.

our sheep were spared the cull that devastated so many flocks in this part of the country.

When we bought the Spanishlake land in 2004 Carl suggested something more cuddly and placid. We chose the local Greyface Dartmoor sheep which is also now a rare breed. They are big and white with long lustrous wool traditionally used for making carpets and their very laid back temperaments make them good role models for stressed clergy.

Donkeys and llamas

Sheldon has been home to two pairs of donkeys over the years. The first were Nicholas and Jonathan who were retired beach donkeys and subsequently retired a second time to the Sidmouth donkey sanctuary geriatric unit. They were followed in 1988 by Hannah and Martha. We did consider changing Hannah's name but she had a very un-Mary-like

gradually built up from the original four to a dozen breeding ewes; all with names and distinct personalities (to Hillary anyway). Hillary shows them in the rare breed classes at the Devon county show in Exeter and one day agricultural shows around the county. The resulting rosettes decorate the Community kitchen. The horns are useful handlebars when it comes to manoeuvring the sheep at close quarters, but can be a bit of a hazard to children. The foot and mouth disease outbreak in 2001 made us realise quite what a close rapport many guests build with the sheep. They received many cards and emails of support during that difficult period. Thankfully the epidemic stopped ten miles away from Sheldon and

to look at, very elegant with big dark eyes, eyelashes to die for, and a way of humming quietly in a sing-song tone of voice when they were curious or feeling sociable. They turned out to be more nervous than anticipated and not as cuddly or placid as the donkeys. Added to this Luke had a bit of a teenage attitude problem, so after a few years with us they went to Cannington College in Somerset to help train the students on the agriculture and environment courses.

Pigs

Pigs were kept at Sheldon when it was a farm, and Mrs Sercombe remembered letting pigs out to forage under the apple trees on the slope

LEFT: Luke and Lazarus with Hillary and Lindsey in 2002.

BELOW: Carl feeding Gloucester Old Spots in the old Linhay in 1987.

personality. When the local farrier retired, Hannah and Martha also retired to the sanctuary where their elderly feet could be properly cared for by experts. The donkeys were much missed by many guests as they would stand patiently for hours to be brushed, petted, fed peppermints and consulted on all manner of life's tricky problems. They could eat an entire tube of extra strong mints without a hint of foaming at the mouth. After the donkeys came two llamas, Luke and Lazarus in 2002. They were beautiful

up keeping pigs. Perhaps some time in the future they will return.

Cats and dogs

Many cats and dogs have shared Sheldon with the human occupants. Cats included Perkins and Ginger who lived in the Farmhouse with Sue. Ginger came from Mrs Pawson, our local vet in the early days at Sheldon. They were followed by Sarah's cat Sniffy who arrived with two small grey kittens. A night of sex and violence with the local tom cat left the

between the Pig Pens and the Copse. During the 1980s Carl and Chris Cockman reared several batches of pigs from weaners to bacon age. Our favourites were the Gloucester Old Spots for their looks and character. They lived in the old Linhay and were easy to look after and no trouble to keep, except in hot weather when the aroma got a bit much for comfort. At that time organic feedstuffs were less widely available and it was hard to find feeds which did not include antibiotics and growth promoters, so Carl gave

RIGHT: Matt relaxing in the Conservatory while Hillary gives Richard Skinner a spinning lesson in October 1998.

kittens dead and Sniffy injured, but a few months later five more kittens suddenly appeared in a hollow tree. Donald and Fluebrush were the two Sarah kept who proved excellent mousers and lived to a ripe old age. Hector and Hebe sojourned here for two years while their owners were abroad – Hector was curious about proceedings in Chapel as viewed by sitting on the skylight, and Hebe loved filling the house with live rodents. Mary Weatherley's two Burmese cats Bella and Bebe also used to come and stay when she did, lending an air of class to the feline community. The latest arrivals in 2007 are Tibby and Tiny who are being groomed for a life of rodent control.

Sheldon's best known dog was a medium sized black mongrel from Plymouth dogs' home, chosen by Jim Pilkington and known as Bootle. Many a school child has gone home from a week at Sheldon with umpteen photographs of her playing ball and endlessly fetching sticks, but without any pictures of their peers, the activities they did or places they visited. Bootle died in 1994 and was buried in the foundations of the animal barn being built at the time. Hillary has had a succession of not very well behaved dogs including Daniel the almost-Old English sheepdog and Matt the failed guide dog golden retriever. When his papers arrived the report

described him as 'suffering from high anxiety and inability to cope with the workload.' Hillary currently has Lady, a border collie with a streak of greyhound in her make up. She has the stamina of one and the speed of the other, but is not very useful with the sheep. Tez and Gail Hastings had a bearded collie called Harley. Simon Lee and Hayley had a staffordshire bull terrier called Levi who was succeeded by Joe, a black and tan crossbred terrier with a lovely nature and an A level in escaping. If you come across clumps of flowering bulbs or trees in odd places, they could well mark the grave of a much loved cat, dog or lamb who has been part of the Sheldon family at one time.

ABOVE: Hillary fetching sheep for Sam Tallowin to shear in May 2006.

BELOW: Showing off our
rosettes from the Devon
County Show in May
2002.

Wildlife

The wildlife with which we are
privileged to share Sheldon is one of
the many delights guests enjoy. Some
species are accessible and easy to see,
especially the birds frequenting the
strategically placed feeders outside
Linhay and Pig Pen windows. There
is a good range of birds, including
skylarks, green, greater and lesser
spotted woodpeckers, nuthatches, and
a colony of long tailed tits in the copse.
Summer visitors include swallows,
house martins and the swifts which
scream in like fighter jets to nest in
the eaves of the thatched roofs and in
the narrow gaps under the corrugated
iron cladding on the Long Barn gable
wall. One can often watch buzzards
riding the thermals over the valley,
and sometimes catch sight of a kestrel
or perhaps a visiting peregrine falcon.
Tawny owls are often heard, less often
seen. They are especially vocal in
January as they pair up and begin to
nest and breed.

An abundance of rabbits and grey
squirrels do a lot of damage by

stripping the bark of young trees or unprotected hedge plants, which sadly don't survive such treatment. Foxes are generally shy but one was photographed checking out the theatre terraces immediately after a concert. Yonder wood has long been home to a family of badgers constantly reworking their extensive setts. A quiet visit at dusk is often rewarded by glimpses or at least the sounds of them foraging in the leafmould. They sometimes raid our compost heaps, occasionally getting exceedingly cross and embarrassed when they can't

LEFT: Roe deer having a tasty snack in the Pig Pens garden and relaxing on the theatre terraces.

climb out. Especially welcome are the graceful roe deer which have become more numerous in recent years and can often be seen browsing in the copse or resting in the lee of sheltered, sunny hedges. In 2006 two does with a fawn each were regular visitors. They seemed to know when there weren't many guests on site and would wander round the buildings snacking on the flowers and tender shoots of carefully nurtured shrubs.

The future

No doubt there are changes required of those of us already here, and challenges to be faced - some already clear, others half-glimpsed, maybe some mercifully hidden. The Community needs to grow if we are to develop our ministry. Are there still people brave and/or foolhardy enough to take on this sort of life? We did not set out to write this book as a recruitment tool, but who knows, perhaps there will be those who are encouraged and inspired by what we have written?

The world does not stand still. Needs change and expectations rise. In 1991 the Long Barn was the best of our accommodation, and now it is the poorest. Fifteen years ago en-suite bedrooms were the last word in luxury, now they are a basic expectation even in retreat houses. So the sketching on the back of envelopes has started for the Long Barn, and before long the sketches will be making their way to the drawing board. The planning and fundraising round will start again, first with trepidation, then with enthusiasm as the project gathers momentum.

As the Community grows, and maybe roles change for founding members as we grow older, more Community living accommodation will be needed. We are not laying down our hard hats quite yet.

The big global challenges and opportunites such as climate change and new communications will surely impact on the way Sheldon evolves in the years ahead. The church is changing too, and with it the needs of those in leadership. We are all still embodied human beings, so stress is unlikely to disappear. We see plenty of need for the type of sanctuary that Sheldon can offer; and for the healing of body, mind and spirit that guests experience here. We will continue to learn and develop our skills at helping people effectively and with care, respect and dignity.

In the end, we cannot know what God has in store for us or this place. We can only try and play our part to be faithful in our calling to stewardship, servanthood and stability.

Abbreviations

ACCM - Advisory Council for Church's Ministry
CA - Church ArmyCSS - Christian Service Scheme
CAFOD - Catholic Agency for Overseas Development
CORAT - Christian Organisations Research & Advisory Trust
DTI - Department of Trade and Industry
HR - Human Resources
ITEC - International Therapy Exam Council
ME/CFS - Myalgic Encephalomyalgia/Chronic Fatigue Syndrome
MME - Mary and Martha Enterprises Ltd
MMG - Mission to Military Garrisons
MMS - Medical Mission Sisters
MRSA - Methicillin Resistant Staphylococcus Aureus
MSC - Manpower Services Commission
NI - National Insurance
NMW - National Minimum Wage
part M - building regulations for disabled access
PMT - premenstrual tension
PHAB - Physically Handicapped and Able Bodied
SMM - Society of Mary and Martha
TYCIA - Teign Young Christians in Action

Acknowledgements

Photographs:
>Sarah Horsman
>Karen Taylor
>David Silk
>Hillary Hanson
>Lee family albums
>Geoffrey Fraser archives
>unknown others

Fat Pigeon illustrations: Sue Ashby

Proof reading: Sheila Atkinson

Maps: Richard Allen

Layout and design: Sarah Horsman

Thank you

Our warm thanks to all past and present ...

- Members of the Sheldon Community and Sheldon Family
- Friends of Sheldon
- Friends of Mary and Martha
- Donors to the Society
  grant making trusts
  individual supporters
  church and cathedral congregations
  religious communities
- Trustees of the Society
- Patrons of the Society
- Sheldon volunteers
- Sheldon staff

... without whom none of this story would have been possible.